Melody Madson - May It Please the Court?

Jodie Toohey

ALSO BY JODIE TOOHEY

FICTION
Missing Emily: Croatian Life Letters

POETRY
Crush and Other Love Poems for Girls
Other Side of Crazy

Published by BookLocker.com, Inc., Bradenton, Florida.

Printed in the United States of America on acid-free paper.

BookLocker.com, Inc.
2014

First Edition

ACKNOWLEDGEMENTS:

Thank you to Connie Heckert, my daughter, and her friends from her Girl Scout troop for reading and making comment during the drafting and numerous revisions of this book.

Thank you also to Midwest Writing Center (www.midwestwritingcenter.org) for "fostering appreciation of the written word, educating and supporting its creators" – and me.

Table of Contents

Chapter One
First Impressions

It was Melody's first day as a sixteen-year old attorney, and she felt like a world in which she was slightly familiar but did not know was about to open up and swallow her. She flung her bag full of old law school books and completed assignments over her shoulder. The shifting weight knocked her off balance and she fell into her car.

"Shoot!" She brushed her skirt with her hands. "I knew I should have washed the car."

Her bag slipped from her shoulder and plundered to the parking garage's concrete floor. She tried to scratch her nose, which tickled from the smell of spilled gasoline on the garage's concrete. Forcing the bag back, she grabbed her lunch and slammed the door shut.

As she inspected her face in the side mirror, she muttered, "I'm a mess." She swept her mahogany hair away from her eyes, picking fly-aways from behind her glasses. Sweat puddled on her nose.

She shuffled sideways to free herself from the narrow walkway between cars to keep her clothes from getting dirtier. A few steps ahead, the door to her new world loomed and she stopped in front of it, not sure if she could will herself to go through. As she reached her hand toward the handle, it clicked and she hopped back just in time to avoid getting bashed by its heavy steel.

"You going in?" A boy about Melody's age, dressed in a suit, held the door open.

"No, not yet."

The boy shrugged slightly and then let the door slide from his hand. Melody thought it was going to slam, but it slowed in an invisible air pillow before gently clicking shut.

"You can do this," she told herself. "It's not going to be easy but you can do it. Just face it head on with the humor and friendliness that's served you well so far."

Melody had been giving herself this pep talk every time she thought about working as an actual attorney in an actual law office ever since she'd learned she would be getting her license to practice law a month ago.

She stood there a few more minutes, waiting for her sweat to dry. Though it was early August, the perspiration was not caused by the heat. She dabbed her nose with a tissue from her bag, tugged her skirt to smooth it, took a deep breath, and opened the door.

"Here goes nothing," she whispered and found her way to Frank Smith's office at Lazlo, Marshdon and Brown. Frank Smith was the Administrator at the firm.

"So you made it!" Frank pulled Melody into his massive office. Windows lined the walls, allowing the sun to stream in from ceiling to floor. "Have a seat."

Melody sat in a grey upholstered chair in the middle of the room. It scratched the backs of her knees. She feared she'd have to squint to see Frank behind his desk, but he sat in the chair

10

closest to hers. She felt sea-sick, not sure if it was due to the dark blue carpet or the stress of the moment. She closed her eyes and grasped the arms of the chair as if she was about to capsize.

Frank explained he was charged with getting her started at work by teaching her the computer system and filling out paperwork. He shuffled a thick stack of papers, barely allowing her enough time to sign them, let alone read them, before he whisked the clipboard away and slapped on another sheet. The life insurance forms had more blanks to fill than the others. Melody stared at those asking for her parents' social security numbers.

Before panic could fully engulf her, she asked, "Can I call my dad to get my parents' social security numbers?"

"You bet." Frank pulled his phone from his desk and plopped it in Melody' slap. When she got Maxwell on the phone, he asked, "How much is the premium for health insurance there?"

"It says here they deduct $50 from each paycheck, and I get paid twice each month, but I'm just going to decline it since I'm covered under your insurance."

"Wow, that's not bad. Maybe I should check to see how much I'm paying."

"Dad! I'm only sixteen. I can't even sign for my own flu shot!"

"Okay, pumpkin, I'll cover you for now, but one of these days you're going to have to start fending for yourself." Melody heard her dad laugh through the line. "Was that all you needed?"

"Yes, Dad, thanks. I'll see you at home."

"I love you, sweetie."

She glanced at Frank to see if he'd heard. "Yeah, you too, Dad." She rolled her eyes at the receiver and thought, *How embarrassing.*

After the paperwork was completed, Frank took Melody on a tour of L, M and B and introduced her to as many of the sixty attorneys, seventy-five administrative workers, and other staff he could locate.

At first, Melody repeated each name in her head as she met them. *Marcy, Julie, Mr. Hardge, Mary, Ms. Brown...* but after a handful of introductions, even Melody's superior brain couldn't keep up. Several of them said, "Aren't you a cutie?" smiling nervously as if thinking to themselves, *Did I say that out loud?* Melody was polite to everyone, smiling graciously, shaking hands, and expressing gratitude for being a part of the firm.

"Hi, Frank. I heard our new high school office assistants were starting today. What's your name, sweetie?" a woman with a grey pin-striped pantsuit asked, peering over her half-rimmed glasses, her high grey-blond bun wobbling as she smiled. "I'm Delores, Mr. Lazlo's administrative assistant."

Frank cleared his throat, "Delores, this is Melody. She is our new associate."

Delores chuckled. "Frank! He's always joking around." Delores spoke into her hand cupped around her mouth as if sharing a secret.

"No, Delores. Really," said Frank. "Tell her, Melody."

"Yes, Ma'am. My name is Melody Madson and today is my first day as an associate here."

"But you can't be more than seventeen years old!"

"Actually, I'm sixteen. I just graduated law school last May. Maybe you heard about it on the news?"

"No, I hadn't heard that. So you're one of those geniuses or something?"

"Yes, but we prefer 'prodigy' or 'age-challenged.'" Melody smiled, making her sea-blue eyes gazing through her purple wire-rimmed glasses perched on her freckled nose as friendly as possible. "That was a joke."

Delores' eyes squinted though her face looked blank. Melody tucked the right side of her hair behind her ear. Her hair was cut into a shoulder length bob and the sides were constantly irritating her neck. She smiled, fighting the urge to scratch.

"Oh, yes! Funny! Well, I'd better get back to my desk before Mr. Lazlo sends out the search party. Welcome, Melody!"

"Thank you, Delores. Nice to meet you."

Delores hurried away, her thick pantyhose-covered calves scratching as she walked. Melody thought she looked like a penguin waddling away as fast as she could in her narrow tube skirt and suppressed a laugh.

"Sorry about that, Melody." Frank said, his face seeming rosier. It reminded her of her dad the first time he had to buy her tampons.

Frank told the attorneys that after lunch, Melody's office would be open for business, and she would be ready to help them with anything they needed.

"Well, I'm sure I can come up with something. Let me think about it." Mr. Petersen strained his neck over the stacks of paper covering what Melody assumed was his desk. His name plate sat atop a two-foot high pile of manila folders with the papers between them sticking out in all directions.

"I have to finish this, then I'll need someone to run it over to the courthouse," said one of the middle-aged attorneys, waving some papers.

"My secretary is gone for the day, so I could use someone to type some dictation and make some copies for me," offered an attorney that reminded Melody of her Grandpa Andrew with his gruff voice and football-shaped head.

"Mr. Killjoy…," Frank said.

Melody choked back a laugh and thought she could not wait to call Jewel Johnson that night.

"Melody is our new associate, so she will need projects for which she can bill like all the other associates," said Frank.

"Yes, of course. I still need that dictation and some copies made. Why isn't one of those floating secretaries here to help me?" Mr. Killjoy bellowed.

Frank's voice rose, "Mimsy copied me on her e-mail last Tuesday saying she would not be in today and asked if you wanted her to reserve a floater. Did you reply?"

*Mimsy…floater…*Melody couldn't hold back any longer. She turned her back to Frank and Mr. Killjoy, pretending to admire the faded pictures of Mr. Killjoy's children displayed on the credenza along his office wall while she composed herself.

"I'll check into it, Mr. Killjoy, and see if someone is available to help you this afternoon."

"Whatever."

"Are you ready to press on, Melody?" said Frank.

"Yes. It was nice to meet..." Melody felt a giggle creeping in when she thought of saying Mr. Killjoy's name, so she ended her sentence with, "you." Mr. Killjoy barely glanced up from the document he held two inches in front of his face, swinging his glasses in his right hand. He raised the glasses slightly as they walked out the door. Melody wondered if that was a salute or Mr. Killjoy's way of saying, "Good riddance."

At noon, after weaving in and out of the maze of offices meeting everyone, Melody's face hurt from smiling and her stomach growled from hunger. Frank escorted her to her office.

"Here we are. Since you're a salaried attorney with no set daily hours but just billable hours to maintain, you can set your own lunch schedule, but most of the attorneys usually take an hour. There's a couple of places in the neighborhood where you can grab a burger or a sandwich if you didn't bring your lunch, or you can go home or do whatever you'd like."

"I brought my lunch, thank you."

"What did Mom pack for you? Tuna sandwich, P.B. & J? My kids could eat those every day." Frank chuckled, rubbing his slightly protruding stomach.

"No. I'm in charge of my own lunch. I brought a salad and an apple."

"Okay…well…you enjoy and let me know if you need anything, okay?" Frank seemed to be in as much of a rush to get away as Melody was to have him go away.

"Yes, sir. I will. Thank you." Melody stood until she could no longer see Frank's sweater-vested back and then quietly sank into the leather office chair behind her desk. She closed her office door, pulled her salad and apple from the pink plastic lunch cooler she had received from Jewel as a graduation gift, and slowly ate.

She watched the cars on the streets and other downtown workers sharing happy conversations with each other on the sidewalk below. They all seemed to have purpose and to be comfortable with their lives. Melody was anything but comfortable. Everyone she had met that morning had made her feel like a joke. She wondered if she would ever be able to convince them to take her seriously.

Chapter Two
Long Afternoon

Melody glanced again at the clock in the lower right hand corner of her flat-screen computer monitor. *4:00; just one more hour to go*, she thought. She thought about sneaking a peek at her cell phone, which was turned off like it was supposed to be, when the ring of the telephone startled her. Her heart pounding, she picked up the receiver, "Melody speaking."

"I have a call from a Ms. Jewel Johnson for you. May I put her through?" said the firm receptionist.

"Yes. Thank you."

Jewel and Melody had gone to daycare together. A few days after Melody had moved into her house, she was exploring her new front yard and spotted Jewel playing dolls on her own front lawn a few houses down the block. Jewel and Melody became best friends the moment their eyes met across the barberry hedges separating the lots between them. Their friendship continued even after Jewel's family moved to a new subdivision on the other side of town. Since they were never in the same school, the fact they were no longer in the same school district didn't impact their friendship.

Melody heard the click from the receptionist hanging up her phone and immediately heard loud music. She held the telephone away from her ear, "Jewel?"

"Hey, Melody! How's your first day? Have you saved the world or got anybody off for murder yet?"

Jewel never seemed to notice Melody's brain, and they remained good friends even through law school graduation. Jewel always viewed Melody as a regular kid and then teenager; into boys, music, and movies just the way she was. Even during her most intense weeks of school and studying, Melody always carved out two or three hours every week to spend with Jewel. Some weeks, it was the only time she really had for herself and was the only time she felt like a normal kid.

"Ha! Ha! I have a couple of stories to tell you but nothing exciting. I've just been sitting her all day, waiting for someone to need me to do something."

"Boring! Guess who I heard might ask me to the fall dance?"

"Not Chad?"

"Exactly. I was at the pool talking to Lindsay who you know lives next door to Chad. She said she heard Chad talking to Marty about the dance. She heard Chad say he is thinking of asking me to go with him. Isn't that awesome?"

"Cool, Jewel. I should get back to working…or sitting here staring at my computer screen."

"Come on. You just said that you don't have anything to do. You can talk for a few minutes, can't you?"

"I guess." Melody leaned her elbow on her wood-grained plastic laminate desktop, resting her head in her palm. She listened to Jewel talking about her day lounging at the pool with friends from her high school. She responded with an occasional "Really," "Hmm," or laugh but that was okay because she liked to hear about Jewel's life. It helped to give her a sense of what she'd missed by speeding through that period in a typical girl's life. Sometimes it made her grateful she had missed out.

"Just one more week until school starts. Junior year! I can't believe it! Then five weeks after that, the fall dance," said Jewel. "I sure hope Lindsay is right about Chad. What should I wear; do you think my…"

"Ahemm." Melody heard a knock. She jumped again and turned to see one of the attorneys she'd met earlier.

"I've got to go. I'll get back to you later."

"What?" Jewel took a moment to catch on. "Okay, call me to…" Melody hung up the phone.

"Hello, Mr…" Melody replayed her tour in her mind in super-speed, trying to remember the attorney's name.

"It's Robertson but you can call me Jared."

"I'm sorry, Mr… Jared." Melody could feel warmth rise in her face.

"Don't sweat it. It took me two weeks to find my way around here and two years to learn everyone's name." Mr. Robertson smiled. "How would you like to save the day?"

"What can I do for you?" Melody immediately liked Mr. Robertson and was glad to help him. *Finally, someone who actually needs me for a real job*, Melody thought.

"Actually, it's not that exciting and I'm sure not really what you thought you'd be doing, but it is important. I just drafted this motion that I need to get out today or I'm going to blow my expert deadline, and I need to finish a report letter to a client before I leave to pick my son up from soccer practice. So I was

19

wondering, will you file the motion for me?" Mr. Robertson tilted his head and winced, "I'm not offending you, am I?"

"No, that's fine. I can do it for you. I'll just take it to the courthouse," Melody pointed at the wall in front of her.

"Yes, just take it to the clerk's office, the civil department on the second floor, and ask them to file it, but you might want to go that way." Mr. Robertson pointed at the wall behind Melody.

"Right. I'm all turned around in here."

"That's okay. Take these and hurry; the courthouse closes in twenty minutes. When you get back, bring the file-stamped copy to Judy so she can send it out."

Melody took the papers from Mr. Robertson. She rode the elevator to the first floor and ran the three blocks to the courthouse. The last thing she wanted to do was mess up her first assignment, and she'd heard the horror stories about angry court clerks at the end of a long day.

As Melody rushed back from the courthouse, file-stamped copy wilting in her sweaty hand, she remembered she had no idea where to find Mr. Robertson's office and couldn't remember Judy. *Is she the brunette with the curls piled on top of her head like a bird's nest?* Melody thought. *Or was it the blonde with all the cleavage?*

As the elevator opened on the 4th floor, Melody ran toward the receptionist's desk, tripping on a rug. "I need…to….give…this…" Melody took a deep breath, "to Jared Robertson," she finished.

The receptionist looked at the ceiling without moving her head. "Okay."

"Can you tell me where his office is? I can't rem…"

"I'm going to have to put you on hold, Hon." The receptionist sighed, placing her telephone receiver onto the brown leather desk pad in front of her.

"What do you need?" the receptionist asked, annoyed.

"I'm sorry. Mr. Robertson asked me to file this motion that needs to go out today and bring it back to Judy so I ran all the way and back, but I don't remember where Judy's desk was."

"Okay. Calm down. Jared's office is just down the hall behind me and then to the left; the middle office at the end of the hall, next door to Mr. Killjoy." *Football head.* Now Melody remembered.

"Judy's desk is the one right outside his office to the right of the door."

Melody walked away, throwing a quick "Thank you" over her shoulder, turning back just in time to avoid colliding with two employees on their cell phones surely heading home for the day. "Excuse me," Melody said, hoping one of the ladies was not Judy.

Melody sighed with relief when she turned the corner and saw Judy, head tilted back like she was getting her hair washed at the salon, peering through the lower half of the glasses on the end of her nose at her computer screen.

"Excuse me, Judy. I have this motion Jared asked me to file. He said to give it to you?"

"Wonderful. Nothing like waiting until the last minute! Typical in this business. What was your name again?"

"Melody."

"Thanks for doing this, Melody. You're a lifesaver! Have a good night, dear."

Judy rushed past Melody and into Jared's office, pen in hand. Melody peeked in and saw her shove a letter between Jared's hand and his desk. He signed without glancing up. Judy rolled her eyes. As Melody walked away, she heard Jared call out, "Thanks Judy!"

Judy laughed and called back, "Yeah, yeah."

Melody retrieved her bag and lunch cooler from her office before leaving her first day as an attorney behind, feeling disappointed. She didn't feel like she'd saved the day at all. She wondered if all those years of studying had been wasted. *I just did the same thing any sixteen- year-old could do*, she thought. As she walked to her car, she wondered whether she'd actually come out ahead at all by being a law school graduate, but she was too tired to consider it too deeply. All she wanted to do was go home, take a bath, and go to bed.

Chapter Three
Celebration Dinner

As she pulled into her parking spot on the street curb in front of her house, Melody marveled at how tired she was after a day of essentially doing nothing. The heat of the early August afternoon swallowed the cool of her car's air conditioning when she opened the door. The blast made her feel even more like crawling into her sheets for a nap, plans that were thwarted when she opened the front door.

"Surprise!" Melody jumped and hit the door jamb. Her bag slipped from her shoulder, bounced off her knee, and hit the floor with a thunk. A banner with "Congratulations" written in large red letters hung across the opening in the wall between the living room and dining room.

"We're having a party!" Melody's little brother, Marky, jumped down the stairs to the landing at the front door between the basement and living area. He flung himself at Melody's legs, nearly knocking her back out the front door.

"I see. What's the occasion?"

"We're just so proud of you, honey," said Melody's mother, Meredith. "We thought it would be nice to celebrate your first day in the real world and Mark thought a surprise party was a good idea. So we bought a cake, some decorations, ordered pizza, and called a few people."

The living room up the stairs was full of Melody's favorite people: her dad; Jewel; Jewel's brother, Jordan; her Grandma and

Grandpa Madson; her Grandma Grace, her mom's mother; and Justice, her cocker spaniel, so named when Melody received him on her eighth birthday just after she'd decided to go to law school. Justice jumped at Melody. She locked her knees to brace herself against his insistent tongue, trying to push him away.

"Are you surprised?" said Marky.

"Wow. Yes, I am very surprised. Thank you." Melody did her best to sound appreciative for Marky. Marky was born when Melody was ten years old. Because of their age difference, they didn't argue as much as most siblings closer in age, but when Marky filled the role of annoying little brother, his performance was worthy of award recognition.

Marky was two weeks old on Melody's high school graduation day. Melody's only other classmate with a sibling as young as Marky was Suzie Sexton, homecoming queen, prom queen, and star student whose parents "surprised" her with a little sister during her last year of high school. Suzie was the poster mean girl, sweet to Melody's face but admiring the sun glimmering off the blade of the knife with which she posed to stab Melody in the back.

It was always difficult for Melody to make friends at school. During her senior year, Suzie did everything she could to ensure Melody would not have any friends. Prior to that year, Suzie didn't know Melody existed, though Melody knew who Suzie was. Everyone knew Suzie; easily the top performer in her class and the only one in her class earning straight As until Melody came along.

At the end of first semester, when Melody found out Suzie started the rumor Melody had cheated on her calculus math class final exam, Melody figured Suzie must have realized she might have competition for the number one academic position of valedictorian after all. Melody didn't care about being popular or being homecoming or prom queen, but valedictorian was another matter. After all of her years of work and nonexistent social calendar, she wanted the chance for fifteen minutes to tell the world what *she* wanted them to hear for a change. By the end of the school year, Suzie had succeeded in alienating all of Melody's classmates from her, but Suzie's popularity didn't count in choosing valedictorian, so despite all of her manipulation and scheming, Suzie had to settle for the number two position of salutatorian, and Melody enjoyed every second of her hard-fought success.

Melody was glad when she was able to leave high school behind and was relieved to confirm her suspicion that after college and getting a real job, it was family and a couple of close friends that mattered anyway.

"Come here and give Grammy a hug." Melody's Grandma Grace held out her arms to Melody, hands repeatedly clasping like she was coaxing a baby to take his first steps.

"Where's Grandpa?" Melody asked, walking into her grandmother's arms, holding her breath to keep from choking on the sweet perfume emanating from her body like an oversized parka.

"You know Grandpa Andrew; buried in some project." Grace held Melody by her shoulders at arms' length. "Let me see how much you've grown."

"Grandma, I saw you two weeks ago."

"Pizza's here!" Marky yelled, saving Melody from Grace's scrutinizing.

Melody freed herself from her grandma's grasp. She went to the kitchen and grabbed a diet cola from the refrigerator, hoping the caffeine would get her through the evening.

"Jewel, are you ready for school to start?" Melody's father said as everyone sat down to the table, supporting their pizza on paper plates supplied by the restaurant. Melody's stomach growled when she smelled the spicy sausage and tomatoes.

Jewel rolled her eyes and smiled. "Yeah, I guess. My mom made me pack my backpack on July first."

Max laughed. "Well, it sounds like she's ready, anyway. How about you, Jordan? Are you ready for your senior year? Thought about college?"

"Yes, sir." Jordan glanced over at Melody. "Actually, I was thinking of going for pre-law and hope to get some advice from Melody."

"Really? Two lawyers who spent their early years on the same block; wouldn't that be something? Are you going to Illinois U or thinking of somewhere a little further away from the nest?"

"I'm considering Illinois University; that way I can live at home."

"No way!" Jewel said. "I thought I was finally going to get some peace and quiet…and a bigger room." She laughed.

Jordan stuck his tongue out at Jewel. "Ha! Ha! I guess I just can't bear the thought of being away from my little sis so much."

Jewel leaned over and pretended to whisper to Melody. She giggled as Jewel's "Psst, Psst, Psst, Psst" tickled her ear.

"At least another two years of torturing my baby sister and her little friend; what more could I ask for?" Jordan raised his can of soda toward Melody and winked at her.

Melody felt a brief flutter in her stomach and mentally chided herself. Jordan was like her older brother. She had known him for as long as she could remember. When she and Jewel were in grade school, Jordan had chased Melody and Jewel around the backyard, growling through his missing two front teeth. When his voice was changing and he would suddenly squeak in the middle of a sentence, he would stomp off as Jewel and Melody rolled on the floor, bursting into giggles, not interested in the end of the sentence. Now Jordan was nearly eighteen years old, no longer gangly and awkward. His blond hair fell into place except for one piece in the front that he constantly seemed to be sweeping away from his blue eyes.

Though Jordan was a year older than Jewel, they looked so similar people often mistook them for twins. Being told she looked like Jordan's clone infuriated Jewel. Though they got along as well as any other brother and sister, Jewel thought Jordan completely unattractive. Melody thought Jewel was silly; she

27

thought Jewel was beautiful and Jordan never seemed to lack attention from girls.

"Now, now, kids. Let's not fight." Max pretended to scold. "So tell us about your day, Melody."

"No, no. My turn. My turn. I want to tell about my day!" Marky dropped his pizza on to his plate and grease splattered as it hit the glossy paper.

"Go ahead, Marky. You go first," said Melody, thankful for the reprieve.

"Okay. First, I opened my eyes and my clock said 6:42 so I waited until it said 6:45. Then I got up and went pee. I put the lid up then I pulled down my pajamas then I pulled down my underpants, my superman ones, then I…"

"Marky, you can skip the details." Meredith sighed.

"Okay. So after I went p…, used the fa…cil…i…ties, my stomach growled so I asked it what it wanted. It said a pancake so I found Mommy." Marky told the story of his day, his hands waving for emphasis, absorbing the limelight. Melody's mind wandered back over the past hours. She retraced her tour of the office, testing herself on everyone's names and the locations of the conference rooms. She finished eating her pizza, folded her hands in her lap, and waited for her mother to encourage Marky to wrap up. She hoped everyone had forgotten Max's original question about *her* day. She had nothing to tell and didn't want to disappoint them.

How can I tell them that all of the money they spent, support they offered, and admiration they showered to get me through law school was in vain?

Chapter Four
Acceleration

Melody could barely stifle her yawns as she visited with her guests. They finally left at eight and she immediately excused herself to go to bed. Despite her fatigue, she couldn't fall asleep. Her mind wandered back to law school graduation and the epiphany which began to mar her confidence in herself and the path she had chosen.

At sixteen, Melody was the youngest person she had heard of in the entire world to earn a law degree, but the intensity of law school and grueling internship left her feeling at least the same age, if not older, than her fellow graduating classmates.

Melody was scheduled to take the bar exam two weeks after graduation, so the following fourteen days consisted of cramming and all-nighters to prepare for the infamously impossible exam. She remembered how finding a job wasn't as easy as the outside world seemed to believe at that time, either. One month before law school ended, Melody had secured the job offer at Lazlo, Marshdon and Brown because they were willing to take a chance on her. But the offer was contingent on passing the bar exam on the first try. Melody agreed that if she couldn't begin work August first, she would voluntarily relinquish the employment offer, and if she didn't pass, she couldn't retake the exam until October. Luckily, she passed the exam on the first attempt. She thought about how glad she was she didn't have to spend the rest of her short summer break studying and was able to concentrate on having a little fun instead.

She remembered the flashes from the press that greeted her as she exited Lincoln Auditorium where she'd just received her JD degree from Illinois University. As soon as she had opened the doors, the reporters, who had let the students ahead of her pass without notice, suddenly shoved toward Melody and thrust microphones in her face.

"Ms. Madson, how does it feel to be the youngest person to ever earn a law degree?"

"What's next?"

"When do you take the bar exam?"

"Have you secured a job yet?"

She remembered she tried to be polite to the reporters as they asked the questions she'd heard periodically in some form or another throughout her life. They were the same types of questions she heard when her daycare, as a marketing ploy, leaked her ability to talk in complete sentences on her first birthday. They were the same questions asked when she was reading intermediate school level books in pre-school and began kindergarten at four years old where she was only enrolled for two weeks before being shuffled up to first grade. The reporters were there when Melody tested out of second and third grade, placing her in fourth grade at age five; started high school at age eight; graduated from high school at ten years old; and completed her undergraduate degree just before her teen years.

Reporters had always seemed fascinated with the fact Melody had always been mentally older than her physical appearance revealed. Though her brain was twenty-five years old, she thought she looked barely thirteen.

She remembered the questions that bombarded her. "Melody, are you concerned about working with people, some surely twice your age, in such a serious business as trial law?"

"Do you have a boyfriend yet?"

"Do you think you will ever be able to have a significant relationship since anyone with education and experiences equal to yours will be at least ten years older?"

"Have you thought about the potential impact of your accelerated life on your future?"

"Are you worried work life will be too difficult as compared to academia?"

The reporters' questions became increasingly personal. She remembered with embarrassment the moment all of the worries she had buried the previous few years forced themselves to the forefront and slapped her with the real possibility that she would always be just an academic anomaly.

You must always be polite and tolerant. For the first time, Melody ignored this directive from her parents. She could not answer another question. She thought about how she had pushed through the crowd, rushing past the press, questions, and classmates, running across the mid-May bluegrass of the auditorium's lawn to the parking lot on the other side. She flung herself into her late eighties sedan and drove out of the parking lot, still quiet – the other graduates had not finished their happy pictures, hugs of congratulations, and promises to keep in touch.

Though nearly three months had passed, those infant feelings of self-doubt were still raw to Melody as she tried to fall asleep. She swallowed hard to keep her tears from escaping. She had done the same as she drove away from graduation, but she was not successful that day and her tears streamed down on her pink fur-covered steering wheel. She turned in bed and lay her head down by a softly snoring Justice. She rubbed her hand over his back and wondered if she could make it all work and, if she did, if it would be worthwhile.

Melody fell asleep running her fingers through Justice's tangled fur. The alarm woke her soon thereafter at six, so she decided she'd take a shower to wake herself up. As she readied herself for and drove to work, she continued to think about law school. Driving made her remember her how the red and green of the streetlights wobbled through her tears and the birch tree leaves seemed to whisper to her through her rolled down car windows as she drove home that graduation day.

Thinking about the birch tree whispers reminded Melody of the birch trees in front of the house she had lived in with her parents, and eventually Marky, for ten years.

When Melody was sent to first grade after just weeks in kindergarten, her parents realized that they would face paying her college tuition approximately twice as soon as they'd expected. A week after Melody paraded her neighborhood in her judge's robe as Sandra Day O'Conner trick-or-treating, her parents announced they were moving. They sold the spacious brand new home they had purchased when she was two and bought a more modest, three bedroom split level in the neighborhood immediately south.

Melody remembered she suddenly burst out crying as her mom turned the key to open the door to their new home.

"Why are you crying?" Meredith asked. Melody began sobbing and explained through her hiccups she was sorry that because of her, they had to move away from their nice house.

She sat her down on the front steps in the shade of the adolescent birch trees. Her mom said, "Life is full of choices. We chose to move to the smaller home so we could send you to college so you can realize your potential and someday make your dreams come true." She held Melody's chin in her hand and looked deep into her red, wet eyes. "Sometimes, you will have to choose to give up something in order to get something else, but if it is worth it, it is not a sacrifice." She said they did not believe in sacrifice and the house was not a sacrifice.

This advice guided Melody through grade school, high school, college, and law school. Every time she had to decline an invitation to go to the mall with Jewel, Melody reminded herself of her goal to become an attorney to help people. She gauged the choices she was obligated to make by their sacrifice quotient. Most of the time, she chose the option which would further her ultimate goal and accepted achieving her goal would make whatever she had declined worthwhile.

She realized in the last three months, her life had completely changed. Until she took the bar exam, she had spent most of her time studying. When she was not studying, she liked rollerblading, going to the mall, movies, listening to music, or hanging out with Jewel, usually posting photos on social media. Now the only activities she could foresee filling her life were working and sleeping. Up until law school graduation, Melody faced living as a child in a world of much older people with grace and ease. Now she questioned who she was and how she would fit in.

Melody knew that even though her parents were amazed by and admired her even beyond the reason that she was their daughter, they worried about her future and ability to handle it emotionally. Until the day she received her law degree and was dumped in the real world, she thought they were just being over-protective. Now she wondered if they actually knew what they were talking about when they told her she should try to stay a kid for as long as she could and cultivate friendships beyond Jewel's and Justice's.

Waiting for the last stop light before her office to turn green, she thought maybe it *was* strange her only friends were her dog and Jewel, her one friend who not only didn't resent her advanced academic status, but relished a world in which she was much too anxious to join. She wondered if it would prove unhealthy that the only friends she'd really ever had time for or wanted in her life were Justice and Jewel.

Maybe today I will find someone to befriend. Maybe they could help me figure out what I'm supposed to be doing, Melody thought.

Chapter Five
TGIF

Hope faded to boredom; her second day at work and the rest of her first week at Lazlo, Marshdon and Brown were no different from the first, minus the emergency run to the courthouse. Mr. Killjoy asked her to scan a binder full of some Plaintiff's medical records and save it to a USB drive, but insisted the digital copy was all he would need on the file. There was no reason for Melody to read the Complaint laying out the reasons the Plaintiff, the person who started the lawsuit and the person suing, wanted the Defendant, the person being sued, to give money. She got caught up reading a report from an operation the Plaintiff had to retrieve a paper clip from her stomach with a long magnet via her mouth. It said the patient had the paperclip in her mouth as she was sorting papers and somehow swallowed it. When she proudly took her work to Mr. Killjoy, he motioned for her to sit the binder and drive on his chair alongside a tower of identical binders. Melody didn't leave the office until 5:15 that day.

By Friday afternoon, Melody was more than ready for the weekend. It took all of her will power to glue her behind to her office chair and not sneak out earlier as it appeared over half of her office mates had done. According to the program on her computer tracking everyone's status, most of the attorneys had left by lunchtime, Melody assumed to catch a dwindling golf opportunity. The rest of the office staff, most of whose names Melody noticed were still "IN" when she was marking herself gone for the day the rest of the week, left shortly after the attorneys.

At 4:40, she decided to take her coworkers' lead. She tidied up the two paperclips and ballpoint pen on her desk, checked her blank calendar pages for next week, and tripped over the leg of her rolling office chair before flipping her light switch and beginning her weekend at 4:45.

As soon as the elevator door closed behind her, she powered on her cell phone and speed-dialed Jewel.

"Mel-o-dy" Jewel sang out when she answered. "This day has been so long! Are you home? When will you be here?"

"Tell me about it. I'm leaving right now. I packed last night so I just need to grab a shower and then I'll be right over, probably in about a half hour."

"Great. Are you hungry? Should I order the pizza now or wait?"

"Let's wait until I get there."

"Cool. I can't wait. See you when you get here." She heard Jewel's speakers crank up before the phone disconnected.

Melody could hardly wait either. It was the last weekend before school started for Jewel, and they planned to spend the whole weekend together. Melody needed a couple of days to think about nothing other than music, the mall, boys, and what Jewel should wear for her first day of Junior year.

Jewel was sitting on her front step, juggling her phone when Melody arrived.

"There you are! I tried to call you and texted you three times."

"My cell is off; you know I can't have it on when I'm driving. Remember the whole rear-ender incident?"

Jewel stared at Melody, scrunching up her face, "Huh?"

"The first week I had my license, remember? The stop light, talking to you, the 'OMG,' then 'bam' right into the car in front of me? Ring a bell?"

"Oh, yeah, that's right."

"Anyway, what's the emergency?"

"Chad called me and asked me to the fall dance!" Jewel stomped her feet, squealed, and then jumped up. They hugged, dancing back and forth, bouncing up and down, screaming.

Jewel, looking panicked, grabbed Melody's hand. "Oh no, what am I going to wear? I didn't even think about that. I was just thinking about telling you."

How would I know what to wear? Melody thought. Dating was an area in which she almost completely lacked experience. She knew her mom and dad worried about her social development, including her relationships, or lack thereof, with boys. Melody's mom tried to set her up with high school sons of their friends several times, but Melody quickly learned that when those boys were not practicing sports or studying for quizzes, they were not interested in stimulating intelligent conversation.

Like most teenage girls, Melody was interested in dating, but other than the few awkward dates her mom arranged, she hadn't had many opportunities. Most all the boys Melody was around the last several years were at least seven years her senior, so her parents did not allow her to date any of them. She was friendly with and considered herself friends with many guys in her classes, but they saw Melody as a kid and were not interested in her romantically.

Melody's sole independent dating experience was with an undergraduate freshman engineering student she tutored in environmental law class during her last year of law school. They went out to the movies twice and had fun, but he was eighteen years old while Melody was only fifteen. On their last date in late November, they kissed. After that, they spoke only when they saw each other on campus. Melody got the impression he felt like he was kissing his little sister, and she was kind of freaked out by his stubble anyway.

Melody started walking back to her car. "Let me just get my bag," she said.

"No, there's is no time for that right now, we'll get it later. We have to figure out what I'm going to wear to the dance. Come on!" Jewel opened her front door, yanking Melody's arm into the house, but Melody wasn't quick enough. Her right foot got caught outside while her body fell inside. She didn't have time to let go of Jewel's hand so they both fell and immediately broke into a storm of giggles.

"Are you okay?" Jewel asked, trying to catch her breath and wiping the tears from her eyes.

"I think so." Melody pushed open the screen door to let her foot join the rest of her body.

"You're bleeding!" said Jewel. "Mom, Melody cut her foot off!" Jewel ran down the hallway.

Melody inspected her leg. Blood was dripping from the back of her ankle. She scanned the room for something to hold on it so she wouldn't stain the Johnsons' white carpet more than she already had. She saw a box of tissues on the sofa table in front of her, but as she stood up to get them, pain shot up her calf, and she fell back down, taking the tissues and the photo frames lining the sofa table with her. She grabbed a fist full of tissues and held them to her ankle.

Jewel appeared from around the corner, dragging her mother, wrapped in a fuzzy pink bathrobe with a towel piled like a strawberry ice cream cone on her head, behind her. Mrs. Johnson held her stomach with one hand and used her other hand to cover her eyes as she slowly approached Melody and peeked at her leg through her spread fingers.

"Oh my gosh. She's bleeding." Mrs. Johnson briefly removed her hand from her face but quickly slapped it back to her eyes as she turned and walked away. She threw the towel from her head back to Jewel and said, "Here, wrap this around her ankle. Get your brother while I get dressed and then we'll go to the hospital."

"Cool!" Jewel seemed mesmerized with Melody's wound, hesitating to completely cover it.

"Jewel!" said Melody, tears of pain rolling down her cheeks.

Jewel's head snapped up. "Oh, I'm sorry. Does it hurt?" Jewel said, and then slapped her forehead. "Of course, it hurts you dummy! Jordan!" Jewel yelled. "Jordan!"

Melody leaned back to lie on the floor. She was becoming nauseated and the room began to spin. The last thing she remembered was Jordan's face leaning into hers. "Are you in there?" he said.

Far away, she heard Jewel's voice, "I'll call your mom."

"Mom?" Melody opened her eyes.

Meredith jumped up, "I'm right here, honey. How are you feeling?"

"Okay, I guess. Am I at the hospital?"

"You lost quite a bit of blood and fainted, but, thankfully, you just needed some stitches."

"How long was I out?"

"Only about an hour. The doctors gave you some medicine to keep you sleeping while they stitched you up. They didn't want you to wake up in the middle of sewing in case you'd jerk around and tear out the stitches."

"Where's Marky?"

"We didn't know how long we'd be so we sent him next door. He's probably playing with the puppy and eating cookies."

"You gave us quite a scare, Pumpkin," said Max. "The way Jewel told it, we thought she had your foot in a Ziploc."

Melody laughed. "She can be a bit over-dramatic, can't she? Where is she?"

"She went home with her mom and Jordan. We told her we or you would call her as soon as we got you back home," said Meredith.

"I don't want to go home. I still want to spend the weekend with Jewel. Chad asked her to the fall dance, so we need to figure out what she's going to wear."

"Honey, you just had stitches and passed out; your father and I think it's best to rest over the weekend."

"I'll be fine."

"Okay. You're a sixteen-year-old lawyer, so I guess we should trust you to make the right decisions."

"I'll stay tonight and see how I feel in the morning. I'll give it a try, and if I start to not feel good, I'll come home."

"Sounds like a plan," said Max. "Do you want to call Jewel and I'll call for pizza so we can pick it up on the way? You must be starving." Max gave Jewel her cell phone.

"I'd rather just show up and surprise her."

"What if she already ate dinner?"

"This is Jewel, Dad, who has the appetite of a horse and the metabolism to go along with it. If she ate dinner, she'll eat again, and if she doesn't, we can save it for tomorrow."

"All right. What will it be then? Sausage, pepperoni, cheese? The Hawaiian special?"

"Pepperoni with extra, extra, extra cheese. My stomach's growling!"

Max laughed. "You got it. Triple cheese for you, Hawaiian for me and my lady, and a slice of cheese for Marky in case he didn't eat dinner at the Kissingers. I'll go out to tell the nurses you are ready to go while you get dressed."

Melody's parents escorted her, limping, to Jewel's door. "Be careful, honey. Don't fall," said Meredith.

"Now you tell me." Melody rolled her eyes.

The door swung open before Melody could get her finger to the doorbell button.

"You're here! Are you okay?" said Jewel. Her eyes were red and her cheeks puffy.

Melody asked, "Have you been crying?"

"No." Tears began to fall down Jewel's cheeks. "Well, maybe a little. I was afraid you'd hate me. Melody, I'm so sorry I pulled you down!"

"No way! It wasn't your fault. It was just an accident. I should've made my feet move quicker."

Jewel laughed and hugged Melody tight. Jordan appeared from around the corner. "See, Jewel, I told you she wasn't going to die," he said. "A person can live with only one foot."

"Ha! Ha!" said Melody. She was used to Jordan's teasing. He'd been doing it every since the first day they'd met. When she was little, he used to pull on her brown pigtails and call her smartypants. He kept it up until Jewel had a growth spurt. Then one day Jewel charged at him, knocking him to the floor but not before running him into the wall. Jordan never pulled on her pigtails or called her smartypants again. Melody missed it a little. She'd always thought it would be fun to have an older brother to annoy rather than a younger brother to be annoyed by.

43

"Does it hurt much?" Jordan asked.

"Not a lot. They said it would likely hurt worse tomorrow."

"That's what happened when I had stitches. I felt great after getting them, but the next day, I couldn't even move my finger."

"You just didn't want to go to school." Jordan ignored Jewel's interruption.

"Thanks for the pep talk," Melody said. "Thanks also for helping me get to the hospital. I hope I didn't say anything embarrassing while I was passed out."

"I just didn't want you to bleed all over our carpet." Jordan tilted his head to the side and smiled. Melody thought he was going to say something else and waited. The silent moment was brief but awkward, and Melody blushed, quickly looking away.

"Enough chitty-chat." Jewel rescued. "Melody's here to see me, so quit trying to be Mr. Knight-in-Shining-Armor." Jewel lightly punched Jordan on the arm.

Melody and Jewel sat on Jewel's floor eating their pizza right out of the box. Melody leaned back against Jewel's bed, her leg propped up on a pillow as the doctor ordered. The awkward position made it even harder to eat. After she hoisted herself up, struggling to stand up without putting weight on her stitched foot, Jewel burst out in laughter.

"What's so funny?" Melody asked.

"You look like a pepperoni pizza!"

Melody looked down at her shirt. Spots of red sauce decorated it and three slices of pepperoni strategically landed on her chest and stomach. "Great! As if I'm not clumsy enough!"

Melody peeled the pepperoni off her shirt, leaving neat stamped circles of pizza sauce and grease.

"Here, put this on!" Jewel tossed Melody a pink t-shirt with "Girls Rule" written across the back in large purple letters. "We'll put some stain treatment on it and wash it before it sets in. It'll be fine."

"What should we do now?" Jewel asked after getting the load of laundry washing.

"I don't know. I'm kind of tired. Maybe we can just chill and watch some TV."

Jewel and Melody settled in front of late night TV in their pajamas; Jewel on her bed and Melody sprawled uncomfortably next to her on her floor. Melody had hoped Jewel would offer her bed in light of her injury, but she didn't.

She had about dozed off when Jewel said, "I'm going to go make some popcorn! You want some?"

"No, thank you. I'm fine." She was sleeping before Jewel left the room.

By Saturday morning, Melody's foot felt better. She and Jewel went to the movies and the mall. The stitches were sore and she limped a little, but she had made it through every dress store in the two hundred shop mall without too much complaint.

They were heading into the fifth dress store, when a girl with long brown hair knocked into Melody, sending her hopping on one foot, groping at the wall for balance.

"Watch it!" the girl said.

"Suzie? Hi! I'm sorry, I must've not been watching where I was going."

Suzie rolled her eyes and shrugged her shoulders. "Well, that's not unusual, is it?"

Obviously, Suzie had not got over being knocked from valedictorian, but Melody tried to make up with her, anyway. "How are you doing Suzie? What are you doing these days?"

Snorting, Suzie said, "I'm living in San Diego now. I'm just here for the weekend visiting my parents." She paused. "I have a great job and make tons of money. How about you? I hear you're still living at home and you're working at that drippy old law firm in town. What's it called?"

Melody heard from her dad who heard from someone at his work that Suzie had recently moved back home to live with her parents after a short, failed marriage, but she played along. "It's Lazlo, Marshdon and Brown. That's great." She looked across the hall and glimpsed Jewel fingering a rack of dresses through The Dress Den's plate glass window. "Well, I'd better get going before Jewel notices I'm not with her and sends out a search party. It was nice to see you, Suzie." Melody started to walk away.

"You're still friends with her, that sniveling baby?"

Melody didn't respond but kept walking away, pretending she didn't hear. She decided not to mention the meeting to Jewel, who tended to hold a grudge. She'd had to practically handcuff Jewel to prevent her from attacking Suzie after the pranks she pulled on Melody senior year. Besides, Melody kind of felt sorry for her.

Putting the scene out of her mind, Melody concentrated on finding Jewel the perfect dress for the fall dance. At almost the last store, Jewel finally settled on a sapphire blue dress, and then, even though they'd just had pizza the night before, they ate pizza in the mall food court for lunch.

When they returned to Jewel's house, she insisted Melody and Jordan, for the male perspective, help her decide which hair style best matched her dress. Melody was surprised that Jordan agreed so quickly. They sat on opposite ends of the couch, waiting.

"Do you miss these school dances?" Jordan asked.

"Not really. You can't really miss what you don't know," Melody said.

"Didn't you go to any of them?"

"No. I wasn't old enough to even like boys when I was in high school. And if I did, somehow I doubt that anyone would have wanted to take me. It would be like me going on a date with someone just a few years older than Marky." She scrunched up her nose. "Totally inappropriate."

Jordan laughed. "Oh, yeah. You're so normal, I guess I just forgot for a second."

"That's okay. Actually, it's kind of a nice compliment."

"That's how I meant it."

Looking at Jordan, she wondered, *Is he blushing?* But then, feeling her own face warm, she stared at the carpet and tried to redirect the conversation. "Are you going to the dance?"

"I don't know. I'm not really sure who to ask. I was actually thinking about…"

Jewel burst into the room before he could finish, her skirt swishing as she twirled in a circle, her hair twisted at the back of her head. "How do I look?"

"Beautiful," Melody said.

"Are you sure? Maybe I should try it in loose waves." Jewel reached for a bobby pin near the nape of her neck.

"No!" Jordan and Jewel said in unison.

Melody pulled Jewel's hand away from her head. "No, this is it. You should definitely wear it like this."

"What do you think, Jordan?"

"Melody is right. This is perfect." When Jewel turned to examine herself in the mirror hung on the Johnsons' living room wall, Jordan mouthed, "Whew," and wiped his index finger across his forehead.

Melody stifled a giggle.

Jordan said, "Now that that's settled, I'll be heading back to my room."

"Wait, Jordan. You were in the middle of saying something when Jewel came out."

"It was nothing. I don't even remember what I was going to say. See you," he said, waving as he headed down the hallway.

Melody had planned to stay at Jewel's until Sunday evening, but while watching Jewel practice putting on make-up for the fall dance, she remembered that she had to work the following day. She told Jewel she was tired and wanted to rest her leg so she didn't have to limp around the office on Monday. At first Jewel was disappointed, but Melody promised to call her later.

Melody went home, read a book, had dinner with her family, and went to bed early, still fanning the flicker of hope this week she'd get some real work.

Chapter Six
A Break in the Clouds

Melody's next three weeks at Lazlo, Marshdon and Brown were very much like the first. She spent most of the day counting the minutes until lunch break and then until 5:00, all the while waiting for someone to assign her real work. She made copies and filed some papers at the courthouse; the attorneys acted appreciative when she completed these tasks, but she had the nagging feeling it was not what the other attorneys were doing their first weeks at the firm.

She tried to find someone she could talk to, but everyone she passed in the halls was either buried in some document or stared past her like she wasn't there. On Tuesday of her fourth week, Melody thought her opportunity to make a new friend finally arrived when a young associate attorney climbed on the elevator a floor above where she'd entered. She smiled and presented her most cheerful, "Good Morning," but he only nodded slightly in response. When the elevator door opened, he practically pushed her to the side to exit ahead of her.

How gentlemanly, she thought.

Three weeks and four days after she started working at the firm, Melody was again making copies, "very important exhibits for an appeal brief," she was told. As she walked to the firm's law library which housed the copier, Melody contemplated looking for another job or perhaps going back to school. She thought perhaps the legal world wasn't ready for a sixteen-year-old colleague and the loneliness was starting to depress her. She was programming the copier's touch screen to double-side and hole-punch the copies when she heard voices on the other side of the library. She couldn't help but eavesdrop. Melody recognized one of the voices as one of the older attorneys introduced as a senior partner, but didn't remember his name.

"Maggie, I need you to do some research for me. Harry filed his resistance to our Motion for Summary Judgment in the Adeline file." Melody felt jealous; she knew the project was important because a Motion for Summary Judgment asks the court to say the party filing the motion should win the case based on the facts established so far, and the other side files the resistance to tell the court there are unproven facts which, depending on which were the truth, would change the outcome of the case. Getting a resistance granted would mean persuading the judge to keep the case open and allow it to proceed to trial.

"Can't right now, Dan, I'm working on Lazlo's Motion in Limine to keep the plaintiffs from mentioning our defendant's criminal record in his trial starting next week."

"Can you at least pull this case for me? Harry cited it in his resistance and I'm not familiar with it."

"I might be able to get to it this afternoon. You can give me the cite if you want in case I get a chance to look for it."

"I need it now. Never mind. I'll get it myself," said Dan, sounding agitated. Melody heard Dan move to the back side of the book shelf next to the copy machine. She heard the scratch of a book being pulled from the shelf, the rustle of pages shuffling

51

back and forth, the bump of the book being snapped shut, and the scratch of the rough canvas covers when a book was replaced several times. Melody continued her 'very important exhibit' copy job. Pull out Exhibit D, copy the records, insert a divider with 'Exhibit D' typed on the tab onto the binder rings, place the copies, replace the originals, click the rings of the original binder closed, flip the pages, clack the original binder levers to open, Exhibit E.

After a loud thump, Melody heard Dan mutter, "Shoot!" She jumped as the bookshelf shook. Having her stitches from the door debacle just completely healed, she decided to investigate. As she rounded the corner, she saw Dan crouched, reaching for a large law book resting face down on the floor, its middle pages crushed from its own weight. Dan's backside hit the bookshelf behind him as he struggled to reach the book in the narrow space between the book shelves.

"Let me get that for you." Melody picked up the book and handed it to Dan.

"Thanks. I think whoever designed this place must've been three feet tall!" Dan chuckled, rubbing his lower back. As he returned to stand fully erect, Melody's head tilted back as if she were admiring a skyscraper from its door to its roof. She thought he must've been at least six and a half feet tall and he was a big man. He looked even bigger in the narrow alleyway between the bookshelves; there were less than six inches between his shoulders and the books when he stood perpendicular in the aisle.

"What's the cite for the case you need?" she asked.

Dan pointed to a highlighted section on the paper he held, 172 Ill. 2d 373 (1996).

"Let's see." Melody found the bank of reporters for Illinois, second edition, a few feet farther away, "Here we go." She brushed her right index finger along the spines of the books, feeling the roughness as she scanned for the 172nd volume. She tilted the top spine of the book toward her and it fell into her hands. She held it by its spine in her left hand, shaking slightly from the weight, and turned the pages with her right hand. It smelled sweet and faintly woodsy, like the one hundred year old book Justice chewed up when he was a puppy. "Page 373. There it is. Do you want me to run a copy for you?" she asked.

"No, I'll just take the book." Dan relieved Melody's strained arm. "Thanks. Dan Marshdon, Jr." He extended his free hand to Melody.

"Melody Madson." She took Dan's hand. He shook her arm forcefully, sending Melody shuffling her feet several inches forward and back. She felt like a kite whipping in the wind.

"I remember…just barely. I was working on this motion when you came by on your grand tour. You sure know your way around a law library. Most of the new associates nowadays barely know what the library is, and when I ask for research or a case, I get back a stack of printouts from the computer. That's if I'm lucky; a lot time I just get a hyperlink."

"My mom worked at the law library at Illinois University when I was a kid. When she had to work the weekends, I went along."

"I see. Nothing to do but study the books?"

"I actually enjoyed it. Every Saturday morning she had to work, I would get up before she did, and when she came down for her coffee, I'd be sitting at the table, dressed all professional. I begged her to take me with her." Melody was surprised at her openness, but she felt comfortable around Dan. He reminded her of her Uncle Larry Madson with grey enveloping his ears and peppered through his sandy brown hair. "I would spend all day looking up cases. I played this game where I just randomly picked out a case. Then I would look up all the cases mentioned in that case until I started seeing the same cases over and over."

"A researcher at heart. That was my favorite part of law school and being an associate. Now they tell me I'm too old to research and have to let a summer clerk or associate do it." Dan smiled and rolled his eyes. "But good luck with that unless your name is at the top of the letter head," he said, raising his voice slightly.

"Sorry," Maggie called back.

"So that's what got you interested in the law? Hanging out at the law library?"

"I guess so. At the end of the day, my mom had to practically drag me away, promising we'd stop by to pick up a pizza to get me to leave." Melody turned her head toward the row of books.

"The good old days, huh? I'd imagine yours were quite different than mine and I'd love to discuss them, but right now I need to get started on that reply. I'm out of the office for a seminar the next three days and want to get this dictated so Ang can get it typed up while I'm gone." Melody knew you only had a short time to file a response to a resistance to motion for summary judgment. "Nice to see you again, Melody."

"You, too." She returned to the copier. Exhibit E stared back impatiently. *Yeah, yeah, I'm coming*, she thought.

She pushed the green diamond start button on the copier. She saw a motion out of the corner of her eye and turned to see Dan's head in the doorway.

"Where's your office?"

"Upstairs in the northwest corner." Melody spoke slowly, trying to picture the directions in her head.

Dan pointed, "Over there then?"

"Actually, over there." Melody pointed in the opposite direction, "so northeast I guess."

"Great. Would you mind helping me with some other things some time?"

"I would love to."

"Good. Have fun." Dan's wave followed him down the hall.

Melody smiled and returned to her copying. It was 11:30 a.m. and she'd have to work through her lunch break to finish the copying before her 1:00 deadline, but she didn't mind, excited at the prospect of doing some real work.

"Thanks for jumping in back there," she heard before she saw Maggie appear.

"Oh, sure." Melody looked up from her copying to see the physical opposite of herself. Maggie was tall and model thin. She didn't wear glasses and her blonde hair was teased into a perfect professional do, parted to the side, rising gently and then falling like a wave to her shoulders.

"Sometimes those guys can be so helpless, I wonder if they ever even went to law school. Or maybe it's the fact they didn't have electricity way back in the day and they couldn't see what they were doing." Maggie nudged Melody's shoulder with her fist, laughing.

"I didn't mind. It was a nice little break."

"Sure." Maggie shrugged. "You going to lunch?"

"No. I've got to finish this by one."

"Suit yourself," said Maggie, passively waving as she left the library. An uneasy feeling crept over Melody as she continued her copying. Maggie seemed nice enough but something about her seemed off. Then it occurred to Melody that Maggie had invited her to go to lunch with her and she had offended her by refusing.

"Great. The only person who's shown any interest in being my friend and I blew it," Melody muttered under her breath, vowing silently to try to make friends with Maggie.

Placing the last exhibit copy in the binder, she snapped it shut and looked at her watch: 12:45. She was proud of the accomplishment of finishing the job ahead of schedule, even if it was just clerical. She delivered the notebooks to Esther English's office. According to the brochure Melody had received at her first interview, Esther was the first woman hired by Lazlo, Marshdon and Brown. She reminded Melody of a circus clown with her jet black hair, pale wrinkled face, and bright red lipstick. Melody held the binders out to her, "Here you go."

"What?" Esther squinted. "Oh, yes, the exhibits." She roughly pulled the books from Melody's hands and dropped them on the floor next to her desk. "That'll be all."

"You're welcome," said Melody, not realizing until she was walking up the stairs to her office that Esther hadn't actually said, "Thank you."

Chapter Seven
A Real Case

Two Fridays later, Melody had just about given up on Dan when the rare ringing of her office phone startled her from a daydream. The phone display said "Dan M"; Melody lunged for the receiver.

"This is Melody."

"Hi, Melody. This is Dan. Do you have a minute?"

Melody thought, *I have a month's worth of minutes,* but just answered, "Sure."

"I've got some work for you if you're not too busy. Can you stop down some time so I can tell you about it?"

"I'll be right there." Melody dropped the receiver and grabbed her pristine new blue legal pad and pen.

The back of Dan's chair faced Melody as she entered his office; she knocked gently on the oak doorframe. He spun his chair to face her; he was talking on the telephone, the receiver wedged between his right ear and shoulder.

"Sorry!" Melody whispered, covering her mouth with her three middle fingers, shrugging her shoulders, embarrassed.

Dan waved his left hand. His right reached to catch the telephone receiver that broke loose. He motioned for Melody to come in and pointed with his left hand outstretched, palm face up, to the chairs opposite his desk. One chair held a stack of brown expandable folders. Melody sat down in the empty chair, carefully crossing her legs so as not to kick Dan's desk. She pretended to concentrate on doodling on her pad of paper.

"I understand, honey. Yes, I know Eric needs to develop a work ethic instead of playing rock star all afternoon." Dan nodded his head at the receiver. He held up his index finger to Melody. She smiled in response. "Listen, honey, I'll see what I can do. We can talk about it later. I have an eager new associate sitting in my office waiting for me." Dan winked at Melody.

"See you later. Okay. Bye." Dan hung up the phone. "Kids, huh?"

Melody didn't know what to say, so she just chuckled at the joke.

"No offense?"

"None taken."

"Great. Should we get to it?" Dan continued before allowing Melody time to respond. "I've got a fairly new file scheduled for a quick trial in about six months. I've got two trials coming up before that one so I need someone to second chair. Do you have time to kind of put this case on the front burner for the next six months?"

"I think I can squeeze it in."

"Super. There might be press involved in this case; there have already been a couple of stories in the newspaper."

Melody took notes.

"There are copies in the file." Dan pointed to the pile of folders on the chair next to Melody. "It's an interesting case. It involves a slip and fall along with a property dispute."

59

Dan explained Lazlo, Marshdon and Brown was hired by the Midland Preserve Our Past Society, who refer to themselves by their acronym, MPOPS. "Initially, the case was a simple slip and fall. A Miss." Dan scratched his eye brow. "The name escapes me at the moment, something to do with food. Cookie?"

Melody picked up the top file folder and opened the cover. "Candace Carstens?"

"Yes, that's it, Candy Carstens, versus Midland Marquee Theater Antiques and its owner."

"Ronald Harrison."

"Right. Miss Candy fell in the building, sued the shop, and they settled. That should've been the end of it, but the settlement included a voluntary demolition of the building. Midland has an ordinance stating any building more than one hundred years old slated for demolition must give notice. Can you guess what happened next?"

"MPOPS saw the notice?"

"Exactly. The president of MPOPS saw the notice in the newspaper and filed an injunction to delay the demolition while it tried to raise funds to purchase the theater building. Simple enough, right?"

"If it was simple, I assume we wouldn't be here." Melody was surprised by how comfortable she felt talking with Dan.

"Very good. You've already won half the battle." Dan pointed to a small frame on his bookshelf.

Melody read the verse to herself, *People don't pay to solve simple problems.*

"Most new associates have a hard time with that. It usually takes me telling them 'keep digging' for two or three cases before they really get it." Dan rested his elbow on his desk and rubbed his eyes with this thumb and index finger, pushing his glasses to his forehead. "Where were we?"

"MPOPS filed the injunction."

"That's right. That's really the end of the story as I know it. MPOPS filed the injunction. Its officers somehow got the impression there was something strange going on. So it hired L, M and B to help it figure out what it is and get its injunction to save the building. Does that sound like something you'd be interested in working on?"

"Of course. I'm not exactly overflowing with work."

"Really?"

Afraid it sounded like she was complaining, Melody quickly added, "But it sounds like an interesting case anyway."

"Wonderful. Take the file there, have a look, and tell me what you think."

"I will. I do have an internet CLE this afternoon but I can take it home and look at it over the weekend."

"They start hounding you with Continuing Legal Education right off the bat, don't they?"

"They do. I thought since I wasn't too busy I'd get a head start."

"Great idea; you should be an inspiration to all of us. Most of us are frantic the last two weeks before the deadline, trying to squeeze it all in." Dan's telephone buzzed. He picked up the receiver. "Marshdon," he said.

Melody picked up the heavy stack of files. Even with her arms fully extended, they towered past her elbows, straining her palms. She hoped she'd be able to get them to her office without them toppling.

"Hang on a sec, will you?" Dan said.

Melody looked up, bumping the stack of files against the arm of the chair. She felt them sway and quickly put them back down on the seat.

Dan covered the mouthpiece of the receiver with his left hand. "Melody, do me a favor and *don't* take anything home. Save that for when you absolutely have to. There's not a super rush on this. The clients aren't coming back for two or three weeks. Check with Ang."

"Thank…"

Before she could say "you," Dan replaced the receiver to his ear, "Sorry about that."

Dan smiled and waved at Melody as she lugged the files out the door. She almost waved back but remembered the files so just nodded her head. By the time she got back to her office, her arms ached. She dropped the files onto her desk. Red indentations decorated her arms from her wrists to her elbows.

She pushed the mountain of files on to the end of her desk. She sat down, pulled the top file, and opened the cover. The pages were fastened to the back flap of the file folder with a metal clip pushed through two holes punched through the tops of the pages. She flipped the stack over so she could read the Complaint.

NOW COMES Candace R. Carstens and for her Complaint against Ronald Harrison, Individually and as Owner of Midland Marquee Theater Antiques, states as follows, Melody read. Anticipation and excitement about having her first real case distracted her. She couldn't wait until she got home to share the good news with her parents and Jewel. She daydreamed of their reactions. She had to start the Complaint over three times and re-read it in its entirety twice before she could concentrate sufficiently to learn what Candy, the Plaintiff's, allegations were.

The first thing Melody did when she got home was call Jewel to tell her she finally got a real case, but she was disappointed by Jewel's less than enthusiastic reaction.

"That's great, Mel. What time are you coming over tomorrow?"

"Noonish, I guess." Melody sat cross-legged on her bed. Justice was curled in her lap and she petted him absentmindedly.

"Noon? That's too late. Chad's picking me up at five. We have to do my hair and makeup. Plus we have to practice dancing and talking." Jewel seemed frantic with worry.

"Jewel, you're a great dancer and you definitely know how to talk."

"But not with Chad! What if I step on his toes or sound like an idiot? I don't want this to be our first *and* last date."

Melody was surprised by Jewel's outburst. Jewel always seemed so confident and sure of herself. *She must really like this one*, she thought.

"Can't you come earlier? Pleaaaase?"

"My parents want to take me out for breakfast Saturday to celebrate."

"Celebrate what?"

"My good looks!" Melody waited for Jewel's laughter. She could almost hear the churning in Jewel's head as she tried to figure out what Melody was talking about. "My first real case, Jewel."

"Of course. I knew that." Melody could tell by Jewel's quick "heh, heh" that Jewel did *not* know that. "So what time can you be here?"

"Marky is usually up every day before the sun and I'm sure he'll be whining he's hungry before 6:30. If I set my alarm, we could probably get going to breakfast by 7:30, so I could be over by 9:30 or 10:00."

"Ten?" Jewel whined.

"That's the best I can do." Melody was annoyed. "I'm sorry, Jewel, but I didn't know you'd need twelve hours to prepare for a three hour dance."

"And the two hours of dinner before."

"Do you want me to come over or not? Ten or ten-thirty is the earliest I can be there."

"Yes, Melody, I want you here. Geez. You don't have to get all huffy. I was just kidding." Again, Melody could tell by Jewel's "heh, heh" that she was in fact, not kidding. "I need you, Mel. I'd be a wreck trying to get ready without you. Who would help me? My mom? She doesn't know anything about dating."

"Compared to my vast dating experience?" Melody laughed. Jewel always knew what to say to turn Melody's mood around. "I'll see you Saturday."

"At ten."

"Or ten-thirty."

"At ten." Jewel tried to sound like her mother enforcing her curfew.

"I'll do my best, MOM!" Melody smiled and shook her head as she tapped the end call icon on her phone. She ruffled Justice's ears and then pulled his sandy-colored furry face to hers with both hands. Looking deep into his brown eyes, she said, "What are we going to do with her?" Justice whimpered in response. She hugged his face into her neck; his fur smelled like smashed up Cap'n Crunch cereal. "Remind me to give you a bath," she said before he jumped from Melody's lap and left the room.

Chapter Eight
The Fall Dance

Melody flung her car to the curb in front of Jewel's house. Her chest strained against the seat belt as she crushed the brake pedal. The clock on her dash glowed 10:45. She pulled her makeup case from the trunk, but she promptly dropped it when she turned to find Jewel standing on the sidewalk in a yellow fuzzy robe and a blue towel piled high on her head. Her hands held her hips and her slippered foot tapped the pavement.

"Where have you been, young lady?" Jewel disguised her annoyance with humor.

"Sorry, Jewel. The one day I want Marky to get up early because there's someplace I need to be, he decides to sleep in until 7:30!"

"Jewel, get your butt in here. You're not even dressed!" Jewel's mom yelled from the screen.

Jordan pushed his mother aside and ran out the front door. The flash from his phone's camera flashed in the cool, cloudy air. "Work it. Work it," he teased.

"Knock it off." Jewel reached to take the phone from Jordan's hand. "Ma-aaaah-m!"

Jordan crossed his arms and held the device in his arm pit.

"Yuck. You can have it now." Jewel turned to Melody. "You were saying? Something about annoying and disgusting brothers?"

"Melody would never say anything so heartless and inaccurate, would you, Melody?" said Jordan.

"Well, not about *my* brother." Melody laughed.

"Touché." Jordan motioned as if he were tipping an imaginary hat at Melody. "I hear congratulations are in order," Jordan said, picking up Melody's makeup case from the grass.

"Congratulations?" Melody asked. Jewel was already in the house, holding the door open. Melody stopped walking to think about what Jordan was talking about.

Jordan must have sensed her hesitation. "Jewel mentioned you got a case at work?"

"Oh, yes." Melody was surprised Jewel had remembered her news, much less told Jordan about her case. "I was assigned to my first real case as second chair. It goes to trial in six months."

"Hurry up! It's getting cold in here." Jewel yelled from the door.

"Cool. What's it about?" Jordan took the opened door from Jewel's grasp and moved to the side of the stoop to allow Melody to enter.

Jewel glared, crossed her arms over her chest, and tapped her toe.

"It's about the Midland Marquee Theater antique shop. I guess it's been in the papers."

"What kind of case is it?"

"Some other time, *Jordan*," interjected Jewel. "Chad is going to be here at five."

"You're right. You'd better get started right away. I don't even know if six hours are enough to make you beautiful," said Jordan. Jewel rolled her eyes. Jordan turned to Melody, "After Romeo leaves with ol' Juliet here, maybe we could get pizza or something and you could tell me about the case and being a lawyer?"

"I promised my parents I'd babysit Marky tonight. They're going out, and Marky and I are going to order pizza in and watch movies. Besides, I really don't know much about the case yet and can't really talk about it other than what's in the papers anyway."

"Okay. Maybe some other time then?" said Jordan before quickly adding, "I'd like to talk to you about law school and just working at a law firm in general, anyway, to see if it's something I'd like to do when I grow up." Jordan looked embarrassed. Melody didn't know why.

"Sure."

"Come on!" Jewel grabbed Melody's elbow and her makeup case from Jordan.

"See ya." Melody waved to Jordan as she was pulled down the hall, trying to keep her balance.

Jewel closed the door to her bedroom, transporting her and Melody to what Melody imagined a model's or actress' dressing room might look like. The top of Jewel's dresser had been cleared and now served as a buffet table. A white fluffy towel was laid out like a tablecloth, and bowls of fruit and flavored sparkling water sat on top. Melody felt a faint mist, looked up, and saw a timed air freshener. *That's why it smells like red hot candies*, she thought, inspecting the rest of Jewel's room with deodorizer-speckled glasses.

A large poster board with an agenda written with a purple marker was taped to the back of the door. Number one, meditate to soothing music, was crossed off the list. Melody read number two aloud, "Practice dancing with Melody." She laughed, "You're kidding, right?"

"No. I don't want to crush Chad's toes."

"Okay." Melody rolled her eyes and continued reading. "Number three, lunch. Number four, make up. Number five, hair. Number six, dress. Wow, we do have a full day. We'd better get started."

Jewel pushed the play button on her iPod. A slow, unfamiliar song began to play through the mini speakers to which the mp3 player was attached. "I found this old prom music CD in my mom's old junk so I put it on my iPod with the computer," Jewel explained.

"Wow. This is really..." Melody hesitated. "Bad," she finished. The girls burst into giggles.

"I know. You should've seen my mom when I asked her if I could borrow it. She got all wistful, sighed, and started telling me about her senior prom."

"I thought your mom went to that with your dad. Why would she get wistful?"

"She did. I don't know. I guess she was thinking about him before his head was bald and his gut flopped over his belt."

"Ew. Not a good mental picture, Jewel. Good thing lunch is not next on our agenda."

"No kidding!"

"So how was your mom's prom?"

"I don't know. I convinced her to save it until I actually went to prom. I told her if she gave me all of her advice for just a fall dance, she'd have nothing to impart when I went to prom in the spring."

"What did she say to that?"

"She congratulated me for being so wise." Jewel put her left hand on Melody's shoulder and took her right hand in hers. "And she said she was proud of my use of the word 'impart.'" Jewel smiled and began to pull Melody in a circle.

"That is impressive." Melody did her best to follow Jewel's lead.

"Ouch. I wanted to practice to avoid stepping on Chad's toes. I wasn't planning on him stepping on mine!"

"Well, it could happen."

"How about we practice sparkling conversation for awhile instead?" Jewel sat on her bed.

"Good idea." Melody plopped down next to her.

The girls finished their day according to the plan. Chad arrived to pick up Jewel right on time. Melody helped Jewel's mom take pictures. Jewel's sapphire dress hung loose over her thin hips and just touched the floor. With Chad's black suit and his tie the exact color of Jewel's dress, they made a cute couple. Melody waved at Jewel and Chad as they drove away. Jewel yelled she would call Melody the second she got home to tell her everything. Melody said goodbye to Jewel's mom and Jordan before returning home. Her parents left for dinner as soon as she arrived, and she enjoyed spending the evening eating cheese pizza and popcorn while watching cartoons with Marky.

Jewel called when she got home from the dance at midnight and they talked until two a.m. Jewel recounted every moment of the night in detail, from the moment she and Chad rode away waving to Melody on her front lawn through the awkward, magical kiss at the end of the date. Melody felt as if she'd stowed away on the date with Jewel.

After her telephone conversation with Jewel, it took another two hours for Melody to go back to sleep. She couldn't resist imagining what it would be like to go out with a boy to a high school dance like other girls her age. At first, she fought the thoughts but then just succumbed to the daydream. It was not until she was swaying slowly in her date's arms in her night daydream that Melody looked up to learn the identity of her imaginary date. She was startled to see Jordan's blue eyes and tousled blond hair. Scolding herself for being so ridiculous, she mentally dyed her date's hair and changed his facial features. The exercise was futile and Melody spent the rest of her imaginary evening with a faceless date.

The alarm screamed in her ear at eight Sunday morning to wake her for church with the family. She turned the alarm off, promising herself a nap that afternoon, but she got busy playing with Marky in the back yard, walking Justice, and shopping with her mom. Jewel called just before dinner to tell Melody she was unable to fall asleep until five a.m. then spent *her* entire Sunday sleeping.

That night, Melody lay in her bed staring at the ceiling in her bedroom, unable to sleep despite her exhaustion. She was anxious for Monday morning and immersing herself in the case of MPOPS vs. Carstens vs. Harrison and the theater antique shop. She finally fell asleep, hoping she was as up for the challenge as she thought.

Chapter Nine
New Friends

Melody was so excited to get to work on Monday morning, she barely tasted her breakfast. She arrived before her office mates and thought the atmosphere was a little spooky as she flipped the switch to turn on the lights. They switched on one after the other down the hallway, like a parade. She sat down at her desk, took the top folder from the stack she lugged from Dan's office, and opened the cover. She found the green sticky note on the side of the page she had marked to remember where she stopped reading on Friday.

A loud bang from the war room a few doors down startled her. The war room was really a conference room affectionately named the war room because it was where the attorneys stored their boxes of documents for paper-intensive cases and it was rumored was where all of the firm's most important cases were strategized. Melody jumped up and went to investigate. As she peeked into the room, she swallowed and held her breath.

"Maggie, it's just you." Melody exhaled loud and placed her right hand flat over her heart. "I heard a bang. Are you okay?"

Maggie jumped up from the floor, obviously as startled as Melody had been.

"I'm sorry. I didn't mean to scare you, too," said Melody.

Initially appearing nervous, which Melody attributed to leftover jitters, Maggie then broke into a big smile. "No worries." Maggie snatched up an empty binder and held it to her chest. "I needed a binder and I remembered I had left one up here when I was working on Dan's last big case," she said, waving the blue vinyl-covered cardboard book. Maggie pushed past Melody to the door and Melody followed. Maggie clicked the door shut more gently than required for the lack of people in the office at that hour and twisted a key in the door handle. Pushing the handle to ensure it was locked, she looked up at Melody and smiled. "So what brings you in so early?"

"Just excited to get the week started, I guess," Melody said.

"Smart girl. It never hurts at review time to have had the partners seeing you here when they get in and still here after they leave. Did you have a good weekend?"

"I did. And you?"

"Sure. It was good. I'd better get back to my office. It was nice to see you again."

"You, too," Melody said. Maggie was most of the way down the hall before she could spit out, "Have a good week," to her back.

With her heartbeat slowed, Melody returned to her office and settled back in to her work. She read the claimed facts made by Candy in her Complaint in the numbered paragraphs beneath the introductory paragraphs setting forth the identities and addresses of the parties.

"On March 22nd, less than two years prior to the filing of this Complaint, Defendant was the sole owner operating Midland Marquee Theater Antiques in Midland, Illinois. On March 22nd, Plaintiff was a business invitee at the Theater. While shopping for

antiques, Plaintiff behaved reasonably at all times, did not misuse the property and watched for open and obvious defects. While shopping, Plaintiff slipped and fell down the stairs between the third and second floors of the theater. Plaintiff was immobilized on the second floor stair landing and Defendant came to assist Plaintiff. Defendant asked Plaintiff what happened and when Plaintiff responded she fell down the stairs, Plaintiff stated, 'Those damn stairs. I fell on them a month ago but luckily only hurt my pride.' Defendant had actual notice the stairs were in disrepair and were dangerous. Defendant did not take any action reasonably calculated to remove the stairs' dangerous and hazardous condition. Defendant further failed to post a sign or otherwise warn patrons of this hidden danger."

Melody next read the allegations setting forth the four elements of a negligence lawsuit to learn the entire situation of what the plaintiff must prove more likely than not are true in order to win the case: a duty owed by one party to another, breach of that duty, the breach caused the injury, and the injury lead to damages or losses suffered.

"Plaintiff has suffered and will continue to suffer damages consisting of medical expenses and costs, lost wages and loss of earning capacity as a foot model, pain and suffering, permanent personal injuries, mental anguish, temporary and permanent disability and disfigurement. Plaintiff respectfully requests trial by jury, entrance of Judgment against Defendant and an award of damages which will fully and fairly compensate Plaintiff for her damages. Wherefore, Plaintiff Candace Carstens, by and through

her attorneys, Siefert & Brown, prays for a judgment against Defendant, Ronald Harrison, Individually, and as sole proprietor of Midland Marquee Theater Antiques, in an amount in excess of $2,000,000."

Melody filled the rest of her morning learning about the basic facts of the case by reading Harrison's Answer to the Complaint telling the court the facts as set forth by Candy were wrong and that she didn't deserve any money and why along with the written questions and document requests sent by the plaintiff to the defendant and vice-versa.

The clock on her computer monitor said 12:05; Melody stretched and yawned. As if it could read time, her stomach growled so loudly she feared her office neighbors would think she'd smuggled a bear in.

She ate her lunch and went right back to work. As Dan had indicated, Candy's case against Harrison was cut short because they reached an agreement settling the case. The Settlement Agreement and Release stated Harrison agreed to pay Candy one million dollars and demolish the building. It further stated how Harrison would follow Midland's ordinance requiring publishing a notice in the newspaper for two weeks at least one month before the scheduled demolition, so objections could be filed up to one week prior to the demolition.

"Finally, I'm getting to what we have to do with this case," Melody muttered to the papers in her hands. She heard a soft knock on her doorframe. She jumped and looked up, hoping she hadn't been caught talking to herself.

Dan smiled and held up his hand like a police officer stopping traffic, "Sorry. I didn't mean to startle you."

"That's okay. I'm just really engrossed in my reading, I guess."

"How's it going by the way?"

"Pretty good. I've just finished reading the pleadings from the slip and fall case."

"Wonderful. This is great timing then." Dan waved his hand and grabbed the shoulder of a brown-eyed, brown-haired boy. He looked familiar. Melody remembered it was the boy who'd almost hit her with the door her first day. "Melody, this is my son, Eric." Eric half-waved. She couldn't tell if he remembered her. "Eric is doing a work-study program at school. He attends classes until 12:30 and then works for the afternoon. Since he's going to follow in the old man's footsteps," said Dan, placing his hand over his heart, "he needs a legal job. I thought maybe this would be a good case for him to get started on."

"Okay." Melody didn't know what to say.

"Eric is a junior and needs to start applying for college in the spring. He needs something practical to put on his college application besides playing guitar and singing with the Heartstring Rockets."

Melody stood up, said, "It's nice to meet you, Eric," and extended her hand to him. Eric took her hand, lightly squeezing it before dropping it and putting his hand back into the pocket of his suit jacket.

"The conference room looks open. Why don't you two take the file in there?" Dan looked at his son. "Melody can tell you what she's learned so far about the case and you can talk about what we should do next. How does that sound?"

"It sounds fine, Dad." Eric glanced at Melody. "But I don't want to step on anyone's toes. If you don't want or need any help, I'd be okay with that."

"No, that's fine. Two minds are better than one."

Eric looked disappointed.

Melody closed the folder she was reading and picked up half of the stack of the file, thinking she wasn't going to make the same mistake of tackling them all at once again.

"Let Eric get the rest of those for you," said Dan, nudging Eric toward Melody's desk.

"Thanks," said Melody.

"I'll catch up with you two kids later. I've got to get some work done today." Dan pointed at Eric. "I'll see you down in my office at five."

"But you promised we could leave at 4:30 on Mondays. Remember that's the day the Rockets rehearse?"

"Rehearse for what?" Dan folded his arms across his chest. "Just kidding. That's right, I did promise that, didn't I? Okay, so I'll see you at 4:30 then?" Dan headed back to his office. Melody and Eric followed behind with the file.

Eric pushed the conference room door open with his foot and flipped the switch to turn the lights on with his elbow. Melody was impressed and imagined what would've happened if she had tried to do that. The picture involved papers strewn over the floor and a multitude of paper cuts. Eric dropped the files onto the table and Melody noticed how they remained in a perfect tower. When she carefully set her files down on the table, the tower leaned and she had to catch the top files from sliding to the floor.

"Do you mind if I take these off?" Eric asked, removing his suit coat and loosening his tie.

"No, not at all." Melody feared she'd sounded too eager to have Eric undress, but he didn't seem to notice.

"My dad insists I wear this get-up every time I come to the office. He says I need to look professional in front of the clients, but I think in all the years I've been coming here, I've seen clients about twice." Melody nodded her agreement and Eric continued, "But I defy him by wearing white gym socks." He lifted both his pant legs to reveal bunched up thick white socks with red stripes circling the tops. He looked at his legs and still hunched over, lifted his head and smiled at Melody.

"Great look. You're such a rebel." Melody laughed, becoming more comfortable.

Melody fought to free the cumbersome black leather chair from the long shining conference table where it was wedged between identical chairs. They were out of scale and too many for the size of the table so she had to almost climb over the arm of it to sit down. After she did, she shoved the crammed-in neighboring chairs away from her.

"They tend to overdo things around here, don't they?" Eric asked.

"Yes, when it comes to office furniture anyway. And I'm not graceful enough to have things so precariously situated." Melody was again surprised by her candor.

Eric laughed, shoving the chairs on the opposite side of the table down as Melody had.

"Where do we start?" Eric laced his fingers in front of him on the conference table and leaned toward Melody.

"The beginning is a good place, I suppose." She turned to Candy's Complaint.

Eric reached his arm across the table, placing his right palm flat on the top. "Listen, before we get started, I want to apologize."

"About what?"

"About my behavior back there, not being very friendly. My dad has been certain I'd follow in his footsteps literally since I was born." Eric re-clasped his hands. Melody looked up to find his expression intense. "Seriously. My mom has pictures of me in that little plastic storage tub they put you in at the hospital wearing a tiny suit jacket and tie."

"Aw, that sounds cute."

"It is not cute; it is sick." Eric seemed annoyed and Melody didn't understand why. *What's the harm in dressing a baby in a suit?* Melody wondered.

Becoming annoyed with Eric's shifting attitude, Melody said, "This case started as a basic slip and fall and, by the way, it's a bassinet."

"Someone slipped and fell on a bassinet?"

Melody laughed. "No, the little plastic tub at the hospital is called a bassinet, but you're right, it looks like they just bought one of those tubs from the discount store and glued it on top of a wheeled cart." Melody feared that she'd insulted Eric, but he was smiling.

"I wonder if slipping on a bassinet would look something like falling on a banana peel." Eric's mood seemed to lighten as Melody related the history of Candy's case. She dismissed Eric's brief irrationality as part of a weird father-son dynamic.

"The parties settled the suit for one million dollars and…"

"Eric! What are you doing here?" Melody looked up to find Maggie leaning against the wooden doorframe with her arms folded across her chest.

"My dad convinced me to work on this slip and fall case at the Midland Marquee Theater," said Eric.

"Great. There's nothing like a good slip and fall case to get your feet wet with."

"Actually, it is more than a slip and fall, but that's just how far we've got so far."

"Really?" Maggie asked.

Melody interjected, "We actually represent the Midland Preserve Our Past Society which is trying to block the settlement."

"Why would they want to do that?" asked Maggie.

"It is a historic theater. Part of the settlement involves demolishing it."

"I wonder why I wasn't asked to work on the case. I assume it's one of your dad's cases, Eric?"

"Yes."

"Oh well, I'm sure he had his reasons and I'd have had to turn him down anyway. I'm way too busy."

"What brings you up to these parts?" Eric leaned back in his chair, crossing his leg and placing his right foot under his left knee.

"I heard there was some vanilla coffee brewed up here and had to get a cup before it's gone." Maggie pointed to the coffee bar down the hall. "I forgot to ask you this morning, do you drink coffee, Melody?"

"Not a lot, but I might have to start. I was wondering why it smelled like baking sugar cookies."

"Do you want me to get you guys a cup?"

"No, that's okay. I'm fine," Melody said.

"It's no trouble and besides, if I get you hooked on coffee, I can have a partner in crime to sneak over to Starbuck's."

"Okay then. Thank you," Melody said.

"Eric?" Maggie raised her eyebrows at him.

"None for me, thanks."

Maggie started down the hall, but then backed up and poked her head around the corner. "Do you take creamer or sugar?"

"A little creamer is good. Thanks."

Melody was explaining the terms of Candy's settlement with Harrison when Maggie returned with the coffee.

"It's still good and fresh. Can you grab one of those coasters?"

Melody reached to the platter in the middle of the table, careful not to bump into anything. She had to stretch to reach the thick cardboard coasters imprinted with gold leafed "L, M & B" between the water glasses and coffee cups. Melody put the coaster down on the table.

Maggie flipped the coaster over and sat down the steaming mug, which was also adorned with the firm's initials. "Sorry, but we have this silly tradition here at good old L, M and B to not do anything to mar the firm's good name, figuratively and literally," she said.

Eric laughed and shook his head.

"Okay, thanks."

"The original old man Brown started it way back as kind of the firm's motto and it stuck."

"So I should drink from this side of the mug?" Melody asked, turning the logo on the mug away from her.

"Yes. That's absolutely right. Now I see why you're a genius," said Maggie. "Well, I'd better get back to work. Good to see you again, Melody. Eric, stop down on your way out today and tell me how your band's doing."

"I will if I can but I've got to get to rehearsal right away."

"Where are you playing next? Maybe Melody and I can come to watch you play."

"I'll get you a schedule."

"Sounds great. See ya." Maggie waved to Eric and then Melody.

"Thanks again for the coffee."

"No problem. Anything to prolong my break a few seconds."

After Maggie left, Melody commented, "Wow, you really have been here a lot."

"Maggie's kind of like a big sister to me. I know at least her main motivation for being friendly with me is so I'll put in a good word with my dad, but I don't mind. It's nice to find someone around here who talks about something other than the law."

"Should we get back to work?" Melody attempted to redirect Eric to the task at hand. "Let's see, where were we? Okay, so Candy and Harrison settled the slip and fall suit and our client read about the demolition in the newspaper." Melody explained the remaining facts of the case to Eric. She suggested they each take a portion of the rest of the documents to review and make notes to share.

They were reading for about an hour when Eric looked at his watch and asked Melody, "So do you do anything besides the law?"

She was entranced by Candy's medical records, so at first it didn't register she'd been spoken to. "I'm sorry. Did you ask me something?"

"Good stuff, huh? I just asked if you did anything besides the law. Do you have any brothers or sisters?"

"I have a little brother named Marky. He's six. I mostly just hang out with my best friend, Jewel, or my dog, Justice, when I'm not working."

"What do you guys do?"

"I mostly just take him for walks."

"I mean you and Jewel."

"Oh. Not much. Just listen to music or go to the mall."

"What kind of music do you like?"

"When I'm with Jewel, we listen to a lot of dance and top forty. I like a lot of that but I really don't have a specific kind of music. I like some songs from almost all genres and eras."

"Me, too. I judge a song by its poetry and how it moves me." Eric told Melody about the band he had formed with his high school friends. She noted he seemed as excited about the band and music as she was about the law when she was in high school. Eric also told Melody about his girlfriend, Amy, and how they'd been soul mates since they were in grade school. He jumped up, transforming quickly from relaxed to anxious.

"Shoot, it's 4:30. I've got to go," he said, pushing the files strewn over the table back together. "Dad wouldn't think of letting me know it's time to leave. He'll get on a half hour phone call and make me late. You going to stay in here?"

"No, I'll go back to my office." Melody helped Eric to gather the files.

"Here, let me get those for you." Eric took the files, brushing his hand on hers and carried the whole stack back to her office. She waited outside her door as he gracefully placed the files on her desk. He flattened himself against the wall of her office and bowed in an after-you gesture, rolling down his shirt sleeves. He tightened his tie. "Well, it was nice meeting you Melody. So, I'll see you tomorrow? Same time, same place?"

"Sure. I'll be here."

"You have a good evening. Don't stay too late. Tell Marky I said 'hi'…even though he won't know who I am."

"Will do. Have a good band practice."

Eric left and Melody sat at her desk. She tried to keep reading her medical records but Eric's smiling brown eyes clouded her mind. *He has a girlfriend and is not interested in you. He was just being nice*, she thought.

As Melody left for the day, she barely noticed the warning in her head telling her it would be dangerous to spend much time alone with Eric. Instead, she woke up her cell phone, dialed Jewel, and pushed her index finger into the elevator's down button.

Chapter Ten
A Discovery

Melody spent the rest of the week wading through the mounds of records and documents from Carstens versus Harrison. Candy seemed to be a frequent flyer with the local medical offices as evidenced by the long list of doctors Melody saw referenced. She wondered if Candy was a hypochondriac and perhaps her injuries weren't as devastating as she claimed. If there was no injury, there would be no case and no settlement and no demolition, equating to a victory for L, M and B's client and the firm. But there was the digital printout from Candy's x-ray clearly showing, even to Melody's non-medical eye, numerous breaks in the bones of Candy's right ankle and foot. She wondered how an ankle could be broken that badly from a fall. It looked like it had been crushed by a steamroller and not merely twisted from a fall down stairs.

It was day three of reading medical records and Melody was tired. She propped her head and rested it on her right hand, the back of her head to her door where her drooping eyes were not visible to passersby. As she read, the words blurred and she blinked, fighting to stay awake. She had just about motivated herself to drag her feet to get a cup of the flavored coffee she had grown fond of the past few days when her eyes were drawn inexplicably to a passage in a note from Candy's orthopedic doctor, Dr. Maerow.

Melody read, *Patient relates she was reorganizing her kitchen and moving her refrigerator when it fell on her ankle the morning before her fall at the antique shop.* She flipped open the binder's rings, removed the page, and practically ran to the conference room where Eric was busy making a list of additional medical records they needed.

"I found something."

Eric's brown waves swung a moment behind his head's startled turn. "What?" Blue felt tipped pen ink scraped across the legal pad on which Eric was writing.

"Sorry to startle you, but I think I found something."

"Oh, no, you didn't startle me. What is it?"

She handed him Dr. Maerow's progress note and he skimmed the text.

"Do you think it will be helpful?"

"Yes. This is great. Did you show it to Dan yet?" Eric seemed uncomfortable referring to his father by his given name. Melody noticed Eric intermittently seemed to act more professional, but she didn't know if this was for her benefit or Eric's father's. At times, Eric had seemed playful and warm, cracking jokes, imitating the stodgy older lawyers in the firm, and e-mailing one liners. At other times, he was all business, mentioning nothing other than the task at hand and the case they were working on. Melody's growing frustration with Eric's behavior was brief; she was too excited about the golden needle she had uncovered.

"Not yet. Do you think I should show it to him now or wait until we've been through the rest of the records?"

"Show it to him now. I need him in a good mood."

"Why's that?" Melody first thought Eric was joking, but then she noticed the seriousness in his expression.

"Because the Rockets have a gig at a Harvest Dance at a high school in Indiana next Friday night. It starts at seven and takes six hours to drive there, so I'm going to need to miss school and work."

"That's great, Eric. Congratulations. But wouldn't you need him in the good mood next Friday?"

"I'd take that, too, but we need to confirm we can do it by tomorrow morning or they're going to find someone else."

Melody felt sorry for Eric. He seemed so bewildered and hopeless when he talked about having to make good on his threat to go to the dance against his parents' wishes. Melody was grateful that her parents had always been supportive of her goals and dreams, but thought it was probably much easier to support your child wanting to be an attorney rather than a rock star.

"I see. How did you get hooked up with a high school in Indiana, anyway? Your band is so good, you're going national?"

"I wish. The Rockets' drummer, Jason, has a cousin at the high school where we're supposed to play and he set it up."

"Well, good luck with your dad. I'll tell him about the record toward the end of the day so it's fresh in his mind when you share your good news with him."

Eric laughed. "My good news is his dropping the bomb."

"One man's trash is another's treasure...or in this case your treasure is his trash." Melody smiled at Eric. "Enough of the clichés. I'd better get back to work." She took the record from the conference room table and turned to leave the room.

"Hey, Melody?"

Melody backed up a step and stuck her head back through the doorframe. "Yeah?"

"That's a great find. Congratulations to you." Eric seemed genuinely excited for her. She ignored the flutter behind her sternum.

"Thanks."

Melody e-mailed Dan about the record, but didn't get a response before leaving for the day. She wanted to question Candy about the refrigerator statement to see if she would deny it or explain it. She would then question Dr. Maerow, hopefully to confirm that Candy had made the statement about the refrigerator as stated in his progress note. Questioning Dr. Maerow to discover the facts in a formal discovery deposition setting would be productive even if he admitted to an erroneous record because at least they would know to abandon that theory of defense and develop one more convincing to the jury.

That night Melody couldn't sleep. She couldn't get the image of Eric out of her head. She wondered if there was any hidden meaning in the way he said her name before congratulating her that afternoon. It seemed different somehow, the inflection of the syllables, mel-oh-dee.

It's like he says my name as a melody, she thought and then smacked her forehead with the back of her hand. "Get a grip," she scolded herself, "you're just delirious from lack of sleep."

When she finally fell asleep, Eric's face invaded her dreams in every person that appeared.

The next day, Eric reported his parents agreed to allow him to go to the gig.

"You don't seem very happy about it," she said.

"How would you feel if your parents wanted you to fail?"

"What are you talking about? I'm sure they don't want you to fail."

"Yes, they do. They told me the reason they were allowing me to go was they hope I'll get the notion of being a rock star out of my system and decide to follow a 'serious' career."

"I'm sorry, Eric. Have your parents ever heard you play?"

"Well, they will now because my mom insisted on driving me and supervising the show, I guess so she can get a front-row seat to my failure."

"Oh, Eric, she's your mother and it's a long drive. I don't think my parents would let me travel that far with my friends without a chaperone."

"I suppose," Eric conceded.

"Besides, it'll just motivate you to give the best show ever. If she sees how good your band is and how professional, maybe she'd get *her* notion of you following in your dad's footsteps out of *her* head." That seemed to cheer Eric up considerably. By the end of the Thursday before his show, Eric continuously tapped the rhythm of the Rockets' songs on every hard surface he passed.

Throughout the rest of the week and the following week, Melody became more aware of Eric's presence. She seemed to eerily know when he was nearby. More than once during the week, she sensed he was in the vicinity, looked up or around the corner, and there he was.

On Friday, Melody was surprised to find herself disappointed and a little sad that she would not be seeing Eric. She was excited for and genuinely cared for him, which scared her. Thoughts of him invaded her thoughts more and more frequently. She watched the clock throughout the mornings and the minutes seemed to pass progressively slower the closer they came to one thirty. Melody told herself she felt this way because she and Eric had become good friends, that's all. She just didn't know if Eric felt the same, if he considered her a friend or just someone to talk with and joke with to more pleasantly pass the time working.

"Hey, Melody, how's it going?" Maggie bounced into Melody's office Friday morning without knocking or an invitation. She plopped herself in the vinyl waiting room chair on the opposite side of Melody's desk.

"I'm okay. How are you, Maggie?" She tried, but failed to imitate Maggie's bubbliness.

"Great. The case I was working on was settled so I've got more time on my hands."

"Congratulations. That is good news, right?"

"Of course. So anyway, I talked to Dan and told him I could work on this slip and fall, demolition case now."

"Oh." Melody sensed her first real case was about to slip through her fingers. Maggie had a reputation in the firm for being the premier up and coming lawyer. There was even some talk that she was headed to being appointed judge one day.

"But Dan said you were doing a good enough job and Eric seemed to work well with you."

"Really?" Melody's heartbeat quickened.

"Well, actually he said you...oh, you mean Eric. Yeah. Dan said he thought Eric was even coming around and would abandon the idea of becoming a rock star."

Melody didn't know what to say. She knew Eric was nowhere near forgetting about his band.

"So what do you say? Can I take this off your hands?"

"Well, it's pretty much all I have to work on right now and it's going fine so far."

"It's kind of complicated for your first case, isn't it?" Maggie squinted at Melody. The concern struck Melody as slightly feigned, but she shrugged off the feeling, accusing herself of being paranoid.

"I think I can handle it." Not wanting to offend her, Melody added, "If I get stuck or need help with something, I'll let you know."

"Okay." That seemed to satisfy Maggie. She returned to the cheerful state she had come in with. "What are you doing for lunch?"

"I have no specific plans."

"Why don't we go out? I've been wanting to try out this new place down the street. I hear they have great messy burgers and crunchy fries."

"That sounds good."

"I'm craving some junk food. Should I just come by and pick you up?"

"Sure."

"I'll be by about quarter to twelve so we can beat the rush." Maggie exited as suddenly as she arrived.

As planned, Maggie arrived at Melody's door at eleven-forty-five. "Ready?"

"Sure, just let me write down the time for my billable hours." Melody grabbed her purse from the hook mounted on the back of her office door and almost had to run to catch up.

Maggie chatted freely and quickly about numerous topics on their short walk to the restaurant. They were seated by a bright window overlooking a busy downtown one-way street. The table seemed to have its own micro-climate caused by the sun streaming in through the old building's inefficient windows. The glass was mottled toward the bottom of the window which ended at the level of the wood-grained melamine table. Distorted shapes of color floated on it as pedestrians walked by on the sidewalk.

"It's like an oven in here," Maggie said. She squeezed a lemon wedge over her frosted glass of ice water, plunged it through the ice with her straw, and drank most of it in one large sip. All that was left was a glass full of ice cubes and a buried lemon wedge.

Maggie looked around the busy restaurant. "I guess we're stuck here, though. I don't see any *other* empty tables. You going to be okay here?" she asked.

Maggie seemed genuinely concerned about Melody's welfare, though she was a little surprised to realize Maggie actually knew she was there.

"This is fine. It is actually kind of nice. It's bright and the heat feels good."

"They've got the air conditioning cranked by your office, too?"

"All I know is that I've been guzzling coffee all morning to try to warm up from the inside out."

"The coffee is at least one good thing L, M and B has going for it." Maggie set her water glass to the side of the table, wiped the puddle of condensation it left, put her elbows on the table, and folded her hands together under her chin, leaning into them with interest. "So, Melody, what's your story?"

"My story?" The waiter interrupted to take their orders. Maggie insisted Melody had to try to the house burger with her with its three kinds of cheese and special sauce.

"Tell me about yourself." Maggie continued. "You're a sixteen year old lawyer; you've got to have a story."

"Oh, that story. Well, there's not much to tell. I went through school just like you but just at a little faster pace."

"How did you like being a girl-genius? Was it fun or was it a major pain in the rear?"

Melody had never tried to put any negative feelings about her experience into words before. Most people assumed being a genius was great and all they ever wanted to hear was how wonderful it was. "I don't know. It was both, I guess. The attention is usually fun but also annoying sometimes."

"Like everyone wanting to take your picture or get your autograph?"

"No, more like everyone's irresistible urge to try to stump me. I have a couple of relatives whose first statement to me before they even say 'hello' is 'what is the co-efficient of' blah, blah, blah."

"Wow. Get a life, huh?"

"No kidding. Most people are really cool about it, though. Some people seem nervous around me until they get to know me a little, and then they realize I'm not a one-eyed, two-headed alien."

Maggie laughed. "Takes a while for people to see you use your powers for good and not evil, I suppose."

"I suppose." Melody began to really like Maggie. She seemed kind and friendly. She felt a little ashamed for initially being suspicious of Maggie. She took a real interest, and Melody was glad to find someone she could be friends with, especially in the firm.

The waiter brought the burgers on too-small plates. Fries toppled onto the table and the special sauce dripped down the side of the burger's bun. Melody panicked briefly as she contemplated how to eat the sandwich. "I'm thinking I should've brought extra clothes today. This looks really messy," she said.

"It's super messy, but I bet definitely worth it," Maggie said.

"Do you have a suggested plan of attack?"

Maggie put her hands in her lap and looked at Melody seriously. "There are two schools of thought when it comes to burgers such as these."

Melody mirrored Maggie's intensity, leaned toward her and said, "Enlighten me, oh great one."

Maggie's mouth twitched. "The first one is called the 'who cares' tactic. Just pick it up two-fisted and bury your face in it, not worrying about the grease dripping off your chin and your elbows," she said. She mimed shoving her face into the sandwich.

"That doesn't sound overly appealing. What's option number two?"

"Number two is more for us classier, well-bred folk, and is the method I employ." Maggie paused for feigned suspense. "Use a knife and fork to eat it like a steak."

"Good idea." Melody laughed. "I think I'll go with door number two."

"Wise choice." Maggie smiled, delicately chewing the piece of burger she'd cut off. They chatted while they ate about growing up, law school, and being a young attorney at a prominent law firm. Melody was enjoying Maggie's company and didn't want the lunch to end, but the thought of her documents waiting impatiently on her desk for review made her feel guilty.

As they were waiting for the waiter to bring the bill, Maggie asked, "How's Dan's case going? Anything exciting?"

"Well, I believe I may have found the proverbial golden needle in the haystack."

"Really? What is it?" Melody told Maggie about the medical record incriminating Candy as fraudulent. The waiter brought the bill; they paid and walked back to the office. Maggie seemed focused on the medical record. Melody asked her what her plans were for the weekend, but Maggie didn't even seem to hear her.

"What does Dan think of your find?"

"I don't know; he hasn't responded to my e-mail yet. It's probably no big deal, but I thought it was an exciting find at the time."

"Oh. Maybe Dan doesn't think it is a great find. I could take a look and tell you what I think."

"Okay."

"I'll just follow you up to your office to look at this fine evidence specimen."

Melody found the notebook containing the orthopedic doctor's records. She opened the binder, removed the piece of paper, and handed it to Maggie. She seemed more excited about it than Melody was when *she* found it.

"This is great, Melody. People work on cases for years and never stumble upon something like this."

"Really?" Melody knew the record could be valuable, but she didn't look at it as *that* important.

"Yes." Maggie handed the sheet back. "What are you going to do next?"

"I guess I should take Candy's deposition to see what she says about it and then depose Dr. Maerow to see what he says?"

"That's exactly what you should do. It's too bad you can't just hide this away and throw it in her face during cross examination at trial."

"That would be great, wouldn't it?" Melody agreed. "Unfortunately, those great 'ah-ha' moments only happen in trials on TV."

"TV makes the law look so much more fun than it really is, doesn't it?" asked Maggie.

Melody replaced the record in the binder with the hundreds of others. Maggie left and she started thinking about the best way to handle the "golden" record. She decided to give Candy a supplemental interrogatory question through her attorney to ask about it. She drafted the pleading along with a supplemental request for documents regarding Candy's refrigerator and any accident involving a refrigerator. She dropped them in the mailbox on her way home to ensure a Monday delivery, hoping this method would provide a quicker response than waiting the months she heard it usually took to coordinate schedules of attorneys and parties for depositions. She thought that maybe she would finally be able to show everyone she was not just a kid playing dress up and she couldn't wait to see their reactions.

Chapter Eleven
A Secret

On Saturday, Melody was pre-occupied, wondering how Eric's band had performed at the Indiana dance. She considered calling him, but didn't. She told herself she would just be a friend calling another friend to see how things were going, but somehow it felt wrong. She knew if she called Eric and he was with his parents or worse, his girlfriend, she would feel embarrassed and ashamed, though she reminded herself if she was just Eric's friend, she shouldn't feel that way.

Melody again mentally berated herself, *Stop being such a drama queen. You and Eric have become just good work friends, nothing more. So maybe you have a little crush on him. So what? There's no harm in that. You're just bored because you have no boyfriend. It will pass and you'll get over it.*

"Are you okay?" Jewel asked. They were sitting on Jewel's bedroom floor and Jewel was again giving the play by play of her first kiss with Chad after the fall dance. The couple had gone out every Friday night since the dance and Jewel swore everything was going great between them. She just couldn't seem to stop fixating on that first magical kiss.

"I'm fine. Why?"

"You just started to stare off into space and your face started twitching like the left side of your brain was fighting with your right side or something."

"Weird." She was shocked Jewel had such an insightful moment. Then, fearing if her emotions were so apparent to Jewel that Eric could see them, she diverted attention back to Jewel. "I guess I was just feeling a little jealous of you with the great boyfriend and me with not even a prospect."

Jewel scooted over to Melody. She leaned against the side of her bed next to her, put her arm around her shoulders, and squeezed. "Don't worry, Mel. Your prince will come." Keeping her head straight, she looked at Jewel out of the corner of her eye. "Seriously, he will. Any hot lawyer prospects at good old Lasso, Marshmallow and Blonde?"

Melody laughed, "It's Lazlo, Marshdon and Brown."

"Tomato, Tom-ah-toe." Jewel waved her hand in the air as if swatting away a fly. "What about that kid whose dad is making him work with you?"

A lump formed in Melody's throat and she choked on her saliva. *Could Jewel tell? Was she that obvious?*

"What's his name? Derrick?"

"Eric."

"Okay, Eric. Is he cute?"

Melody pretended to ponder the question. "I guess some people might say he's attractive."

"But not you?" Jewel took her arm off Melody's shoulder and crossed them in front of her chest. "Since when do you not notice cute boys?"

"I don't know, Jewel. The only thing Eric and I have in common is that we're both sixteen."

"So. The only thing we have in common is that we're both sixteen." Jewel stuck out her lower lip, pouting.

Melody jabbed Jewel with her elbow. "Oh, stop it. You know we have more in common than that."

"Nothing other than we both like the mall, the same music, boys, rollerblading, makeup, and dancing."

"You're right. Why are we friends again?" Melody tilted her ear to her shoulder and squinted at Jewel.

"Ha, ha."

"Eric is into rock music and has a girlfriend. Besides, we work together; it's unethical."

"Who's saying unethical? I'm just saying you should go out to the movies a few times."

"Let's drop it, okay?" Melody was not sure why she was reluctant to share her true feelings about Eric with Jewel. She usually told Jewel everything. They knew everything about each other, from the moment they started their periods to the brand of deodorant each preferred. She told herself she held back from Jewel because there was really nothing to tell. She promised herself she would tell Jewel everything as soon as she figured out what was going on; as soon as she settled this battle constantly stirring within.

"Sure. What else is going on at work? Have you made any other friends?"

"Actually, I had lunch with another associate attorney yesterday, Maggie."

"How old is Maggie?"

"I don't know. I think she must be in her mid-twenties; she's only been out of law school a couple of years, but she's already working with the most senior attorneys."

"So are you, aren't you? Isn't this Dan guy in the name of the place?"

"That's Dan's dad, but he is kind of up there on the letterhead."

"See. You should be proud."

The girls grew tired of sitting in Jewel's bedroom listening to the same playlists and decided to go walk around the mall. They hoped they'd discover someone new whose CD they could buy and add to Jewel's mp3 library. Though she could always buy her songs on her phone, Jewel preferred to have a CD for a backup when she could get one. Melody was so insistent on avoiding the subject of Eric that she kept talking about Maggie. She sensed that Jewel was getting annoyed, but she couldn't help herself. After again mentioning something Maggie had said during lunch yesterday, Jewel jumped in front of Melody, facing her, nearly inviting herself to be trampled, first by Melody and then by all of the shoppers on Melody's heels.

"Jewel. You're going to get us run over."

Jewel folded her arms in front of her chest, stuck her Capri-panted leg to the side, and tapped her flip-flopped foot. The other mall shoppers tried to get around the girls, bumping them with their shopping bags and purses. Melody thought Jewel was joking, but when she heard a white-haired old lady scuffling by leaning on her walker mumble, "Kids today are so rude," and Jewel still

103

hadn't said anything, she asked, "What is going on? The old ladies are going to start beating us with their canes." The lady with the walker's head snapped back and she glared at Melody.

"So I guess you have a new best friend now."

"What are you talking about?"

"For the last three hours it's been nothing but 'Maggie this,' 'Maggie that.' And the way you were acting earlier being all secretive, I figured it out."

"Figured what out?"

"I know what you're trying to tell me." Melody just rolled her eyes. "You're trying to tell me you have a new best friend and don't want me anymore." Jewel twirled on the heel of the foot she'd been tapping and walked away. The shoppers filled in the space between them like the water fills in the trench when you run your finger through the sand on the beach at the saturated edge of a lake.

"You're being ridiculous, Jewel!" But Jewel was whisked so far ahead in the crowd, she could no longer see her head bobbing. "Jewel!" Melody yelled, but either Jewel didn't hear her or was ignoring her because she didn't see any sudden shift in the crowd like she'd seen when Jewel pounced on her moments before.

"Well, you asked!" Melody turned and stomped away in the opposite direction. She kept getting pushed back as the tears welled up in her eyes. The bags, purses, and joined hands of other shopping teenagers knocked her back and nearly off balance.

With her tears so thick, the mall was just a blur; Melody worked her way over to the side of the hall and plopped down on a vinyl-covered bench. The air swished out between the seams. Thinking of how she and Jewel used to bounce up and down on her mom's old faux leather couch just to hear the air burst out, laughing hysterically, she began to sob. Her tears came in waves and the mucus running down the back of her throat from her overactive nose made her cough. Peoples' sacks hit her knees and they were beginning to hurt. She brought her feet up to the seat of the bench, folded her forearms across her propped up knees, buried her head in the pillow of her crossed arms, and thought, *Why is everything so screwed up?*

After an hour had passed, the last of Melody's tears were wrung from her eyes, and she assumed Jewel must have found someone to take her home. The skylight above her was beginning to darken and the herds of shoppers had dwindled. Melody turned on the bench, put her feet to the floor, and looked up. Her reflection in the store's plate glass window across the hall would have started her crying again if she'd had any tears left. Her face looked like a raccoon's. Her cheeks were red; her eyes swollen and bloodshot behind her tear-stained glasses. Melody took them off and began to wipe the lenses with her t-shirt when she saw a familiar blur coming toward her.

She put on her glasses and saw it was Jewel, her forearms weighted down with several shopping bags. Melody put her palms together, wedged them between her knees, and looked down at the floor.

"There you are. I've been looking all over for you. Where have you been?"

Melody looked up at Jewel. She didn't know what to say. She wondered why she should be so surprised at Jewel's insensitivity and thought that maybe she'd outgrown Jewel's friendship.

Jewel dropped her shopping sacks at the end of the bench on the floor. "I was afraid you'd left without me and I was going to owe Jordan big time for having to come get me."

"No. I've been here since you stormed off."

"Oh, yeah. Hey, Mel, I'm sorry. I found such great deals I don't even remember what we were arguing about."

Melody reminded her, "You accused me of dumping you."

"Right." Jewel pushed Melody down the bench as she sat down. She pushed her hand behind Melody's arms and locked their elbows. "I guess I was just jealous. You have this cool new job and cool new friends. You kept talking about Maggie." She scrunched her face and stuck out her tongue like she'd had a bad taste in her mouth. "I felt left out and I overreacted. I'm sorry. Can you forgive me?"

"You asked me to tell you about work, but I guess I went on a little bit about Maggie. I'm sorry, too." Melody tightened the lock in their elbows. "How can you even question our friendship?"

"You know me, Mel. Head of the Thespian Society, certified drama queen?"

"Oh, yeah." Melody shook her head and bumped shoulders with Jewel.

"Remember this?" Jewel stood slightly, lifted her legs, and plopped back down on the bench.

"I remember." The girls laughed. Melody stood and grabbed Jewel's hand, pulling her to stand from the bench. "Come on. Let's go. Aren't you starving?"

"No, I'm okay." Jewel tried to sound nonchalant.

"Jewel." Melody stopped, placing her hands on her hips. "You ate?"

Jewel sunk her head into her shoulders, wincing. "I just had a teeny, tiny pretzel."

Melody looked up at the ceiling and then turned and walked away, again shaking her head at Jewel's antics. Jewel skipped toward her, the corner of her "brown bag" stabbing Melody's calf.

"I got you something." Jewel changed the subject. She said, "It's in one of these," giving Melody the handles of three of her sacks, "but we'll find it at home."

Melody laughed at Jewel's manipulation to get her to carry her bags for her.

"I really did get you something," Jewel said.

Chapter Twelve
In-Service Day

Melody's feelings for Eric and her uneasiness continued growing. She alternately avoided and sought him out. It became like an addiction. She would avoid him for as long as she could, only communicate with him about the case, and only if absolutely necessary. When she couldn't stand it any longer, she searched for a question about the case to ask and used the opportunity to ask him about his weekend, his band, or his girlfriend. The pendulum in her mind kept swinging from believing she was in love with Eric to thinking the best thing to do was not have anything to do with him. The amount of time it balanced on a rational feeling of professional friendship became increasingly brief to the point where Melody sometimes thought she was losing her mind.

And Eric's behavior didn't help any, either. Some days he seemed friendly, some days overly so, and some days he seemed cold. One day when he had a question about a judge's choice of language in an appeals case about historic preservation mixed in with the documents delivered with MPOPS' organizational file, he got a little close. "Sit down here and I'll show you what I mean," he said, grabbing the edge of table on either side of Melody. He leaned in, nearly placing his chin on her shoulder and whispered in her ear, "What exactly does it mean when it talks about eminent domain?"

"Usually it means the government taking property but let me read it quick," she waited for her arm hairs to lie back down and her concentration to return. She thought she heard Eric suck in deep through his nose. *Is he smelling me?* she thought. Before she could decide, he moved away and sat down in a chair across the table. The thoughts running through her mind made it difficult to focus, but she pretended to read long enough to form what she hoped was an intelligent answer. "This case talks about using eminent domain for redevelopment and revitalization. It's discussing the question of what qualifies as a public purpose for taking a person's private property for government use."

"Oh." Eric stared out the window. Assuming he lost interest, Melody went back to work reading documents. The next day, Eric barely spoke to her, though she heard him talking animatedly with Maggie in the hallway as they walked past her office. The day after that, he was back to his usually self, friendly and joking around.

By the time MPOPS versus Candace Carstens versus Ronald Harrison and Midland Marquee Theater Antiques was two months old, Candy had evaded answering the supplemental questions Melody had sent, so her deposition and Ron's were scheduled to begin next week. Dan had to go out of town for a month for an out of state trial, so he assigned taking the depositions to Melody. He suggested Eric and Melody work together on an outline of questions to ask and then e-mail it to him to revise. Eric's school had an in-service day on Tuesday, so they'd planned to meet to go through all of documents again to formulate the deposition outline.

Jewel's school had an in-service day that day as well as the next, and Jewel became angry when Melody told her she couldn't take time off from work to hang out with her. But she was actually grateful for Jewel's anger. It was a welcome, though weak, distraction from her anxiety about spending an entire day with Eric. She spent more time fixing her hair and choosing her outfit that morning than usual and reproached herself for acting like they were going on a date.

Melody went to work early. She wanted to get all of the binders and files to the conference room before Eric arrived at eight-thirty, so he wouldn't have to see her sweat and struggle. She carried them in one by one and laid them out in a long row on the table. She had a fresh legal pad with a new pen along the top binding in front of her at eight twenty-nine. She waited and watched the clock; the minute hand jumped two minutes ahead and then bounced back to the correct time of eight thirty, then eight thirty-one, and eight thirty-two. Melody brought up the calendar on her phone to confirm the meeting was today. She wondered if she should start without Eric. After all, she would be the one questioning the witnesses at the deposition and she didn't really *need* his help. She decided to get a cup of coffee. When she returned, Eric had still not arrived so she began re-reading Candy's Complaint, jotting ideas of questions to ask as she read.

Brainstorming had always been a strength for Melody and within minutes, she had an entire piece of legal paper of potential questions. She had torn the sheet from the pad and flipped it over to begin filling in the back when Eric arrived. He rushed into the room and flung his jacket into the corner behind Chester, the room's resin skeleton gatekeeper.

"Sorry I'm late."

Melody glanced at the clock: 9:09. "No problem. I was just brainstorming some questions while I review the documents."

Eric pulled the chair next to Melody away from the table and sat down. "My alarm didn't go off so I overslept. I know I set it last night."

"Maybe you turned it off in your dreams."

"That's what I'm thinking." Eric leaned into his right hand, his right elbow resting on the table. He rested his left hand on his left knee. His brown curls were intertwined in his fingers. Melody sucked in a short breath, tickling her throat. She was afraid she was going to start coughing, but Eric didn't seem to notice. "My theory is since I didn't have school, I woke up in the night, saw my alarm was set, and thinking today was Saturday, I turned it off."

"Good detective work, but now we've got real work to do." Melody pushed the notes she had taken in front of Eric. "Here's what I've thought of so far. Do you want to look at them and add anything I might be missing?"

"Yes, ma'am." Eric saluted Melody with his left hand, pulled his chair closer to the table, and stiffened his back like a soldier. Melody laughed.

The next three hours were easy. Melody and Eric studied all the documents, comfortably discussed questions for the depositions, and speculated as to how the deponents might respond. Every so often, maybe once or twice each hour, Eric allowed his binder or folder to fall to the table and dropped his pen onto his paper. He leaned back against the buttoned leather back of the chair and asked Melody about her weekend, Marky, and her parents. Though she didn't ask, Eric also chatted about school and his band.

This was the kind of situation which had so frustrated Melody over the past weeks. At these times, everything between her and Eric felt right. They were friends working together pleasantly. Comfortably. It was later, in the quiet as she tried to fall asleep when the disturbing thoughts and feelings would set in. She found herself scrutinizing Eric's every word and mannerism for a clue as to how he really felt about her. The more she tried to push the thoughts away, the more they persisted until she was questioning her sanity.

Her stomach rumbled and as if he'd heard it, Eric said, "I'm ready for lunch. I'm usually not around at lunch time. What's good?"

"It depends on what you're hungry for."

"At this point I could eat anything. What do you normally do for lunch?"

"Most of the time, I bring my lunch, but Maggie and I went to Hank's for burgers once."

"I'm thinking pizza."

"I thought you said you could eat anything."

"Well, I changed my mind."

"There's the Dough Stop down the street. My dad took me to it once a few years ago. It was good then."

"That sounds great."

"Enjoy." Melody turned back to her work and tapped her pen against her cheek.

"You coming?" Melody looked up. Eric pushed his arm through his jacket sleeve. "You are not so abnormal that you don't like pizza, are you?"

"Of course I like pizza." Melody squinted at Eric, feigning annoyance. "And I'm not AB-normal. I just brought my lunch today."

"So."

"So I don't want to waste it."

"I'll buy your pizza and besides, your lunch will last until tomorrow." Eric got down on one knee, clasped his hands, and shook them in front of his face. "Please, please, please. Don't make me eat alone."

"Okay, okay," Melody laughed. Eric walked on his knees toward the door. "Get up. You look ridiculous."

"Yes, ma'am." Eric rubbed his knees. "Ouch. That hurts. Please don't make me beg again."

"I didn't make you do anything," said Melody as Eric took hold of her elbow.

Melody wondered if Eric had kept his hand on her elbow for a significantly long time and if he did, what it meant. He pushed the down button for the elevator and when the door creaked open, he motioned Melody in ahead of him. She became acutely aware of Eric's physical presence; she swore she could feel tiny jolts of electricity emanating from him. Goosebumps took over her arms and she hoped he could not hear her heart beating. It was deafening in her ears.

They were quiet as they walked to the restaurant; just glanced at each other and smiled a few times. Eric held the door open for Melody there as well. The yeasty odor of baking dough hit them immediately. Melody's heart raced. *This is not a date*, she repeated in her head.

They looked up at the menu board. Melody stood slightly behind Eric and the front of her shoulder brushed up against the sleeve of his jacket. She resisted the urge to lay her head on his shoulder.

"So, what do you think?" Eric looked over to Melody. "I think I'm going to do the slice and a soda deal."

"Sounds good. I think I'll do that, too."

The first person in line left the counter, balancing her paper plate holding her pizza slice on top of her beverage cup. Eric and Melody stepped forward.

"What kind are you getting?" Eric asked.

"Cheese."

"Wowee. You are such a rebel."

"Yeah, well, they did call me the wild girl back in the day."

"Wild girl, huh? What happened to you?"

"You know. When I hit ten I decided riding my bike in full leathers and tattoos was too juvenile so I grew up."

"So you should be hitting your mid-life crisis pretty soon then, right?" Though they kept up their light banter, Melody thought how accurate Eric really was. She kind of felt like she *was* having a mid-life crisis.

"Hey, you two." A woman Melody vaguely recognized from work turned from the order counter and walked past them with a Styrofoam to-go box and a giant fountain soda. "You working long enough to get a lunch break today, Eric?"

"Yes, ma'am."

She pointed her cup at Melody, "Eric's such a nice boy. He's going to follow in his father's footsteps." Melody smiled slightly and nodded.

The woman said, "Well, you two enjoy," winking at them.

Warmth flushed through Melody and she could feel a wave of red rush over her cheeks. She tried to dismiss the feeling that she had just been caught shopping when she was supposed to be home from school sick.

Eric approached the counter. "I'll have a slice of all meat and a drink. She'd like a slice of cheese and a drink as well." Melody unzipped her purse. "What are you doing? I told you I'd buy," Eric said.

"That's okay. I've got mine."

"No, I said I'll pay so I'll pay." Eric gave a twenty dollar bill to the clerk. "I insist." When Eric smiled at her, Melody thought she saw him wink but told herself he probably just had something in his eye. Eric was quiet as they waited for their pizza. Whatever easy comfort flowing between them minutes before was stolen by the woman from the office.

They took their pizza and cups from the clerk. Melody had to concentrate to avoid disaster as she tried to hold on to her flimsy paper plate of pizza with one hand and tried to fill her cup at the fountain soda machine next to the order window with the other. After accomplishing the task successfully, she joined Eric at the two-person table in the corner of the dining room. He looked up at her and smiled absently when she sat down.

They ate in silence for a few moments before Melody asked, "So how's your pizza?"

"It's good, thanks." Eric stared down at his plate.

"The cheese is good, too."

"I'm sorry, Melody. I meant it's good, thanks. How's yours?" Eric dropped his plastic fork on his pizza, tipped his chair up on its back legs, and rubbed his forehead.

"What's wrong?"

"Nothing, I'm fine." Eric let the front legs of his chair fall back to the floor.

"Are you sure? I feel like I'm eating lunch by myself."

"No, I'm not sure." Eric rested his chin in his palm. "I'm just thinking about what Carolyn said."

Melody tried to lighten the mood. "Was it what she said about you being a nice boy or enjoying your lunch that bothered you?"

Eric was serious. "No, it was the part about following in my father's footsteps."

"I was just kidding." Melody mentally slapped her forehead for sounding like an insensitive jerk. "I don't think she meant anything by it. She only knows what your dad tells her."

"I know, but I get so tired of everyone else telling me how to live my life. They assume I have the brains and dedication to be an attorney like my dad."

"I'm sure you do have what it takes to be an attorney, Eric. The problem is people assuming you want to."

"I suppose. I guess it is easier to believe the reason I might not become a lawyer is because I can't rather than that I chose to disappoint my parents."

"I don't think your desire to not go into law has anything to do with defying your parents."

"But that's what I'd be doing. I really don't have any choice."

"Eric, I'm sure you know that is not true. You always have a choice. The options won't always be ideal but you still have to choose. Doing nothing is even a choice."

"But it is my dad's dream to have me come work with him and carry on the Marshdon legacy. How can I take that away from him?"

"You're not taking anything away from him. You are taking something for yourself." Eric didn't seem convinced, and it hurt Melody to see someone on the verge of throwing away what he wanted for his own life. "It's your life, Eric. Your parents might be disappointed, but they would get over it. You're their son. Dan doesn't seem the type to disown his own son because of a career choice. The important thing is to be true to yourself. You'll always regret it if you deny who you really are. One day, the truth will come out and it might be too late to go back."

Eric didn't respond. Melody ate her now-cold pizza, the cheese no longer moist and stringy, but dried out and rubbery. "I'm sorry. The last thing I'm sure you want to hear is a lecture. It's just…"

Eric didn't let her finish, "I know you're right. I just don't know how to tell them."

"Maybe you should just spit it out; rip it off like a Band-aid and get it over with." They finished their pizza without further conversation, but Melody felt more at ease knowing it wasn't something she had said that had frustrated Eric.

The rest of the day passed the same way. By the end of Eric's work day, Melody had a comprehensive outline of questions to ask Candy and Ron at their depositions. Eric participated in the discussion and was helpful, but Melody could tell his mind was somewhere else. She knew he was thinking about his own big issues and didn't care much about the Midland Marquee Theater right then. She wished there was something she could do to help, but, like she told Eric, it was his choice and only he could make it.

Chapter Thirteen
Battling

Late the next day, Melody read through her list of deposition questions, tweaking them one last time before leaving. As she got to the last questions, Jewel ran in.

"Surprise!"

"Jewel, what are you doing here?"

"I came to surprise you."

Melody rolled her eyes. "Obviously. But why here? I'm about ready to leave for the day."

"I wanted to see where you work. And," she pulled a white lunch sack from behind her back, "give you this."

Taking the sack, translucent from whatever was inside, Melody carefully opened the top. She was immediately hit with the smell of vanilla buttercream frosting. "This isn't from…"

"Cupcake King! Yes."

"Aw, thanks, Jewel. But what's the occasion other than another day off from school?" Melody peeled the silver wrapper from the chocolate cupcake and took a huge bite, dipping the tip of her nose in the thick frosting on top.

Jewel laughed. "I felt kind of bad for getting upset with you when you couldn't take off work to spend the day with me yesterday so, of course, I went to the mall to make myself feel better. I saw the cupcakes in the window at Cupcake King and decided to get one for you. How is it?"

Melody tried to say, "Yummy," but it came out muffled and bits of cake spit out of her mouth. She looked around her desk. "A napkin would be good, though."

Jewel jumped up. "I'll get you some paper towels. Where's the bathroom?"

With her free hand, Melody pointed down the hall.

"I'll be right back."

While she waited for Jewel to return, Melody devoured the rest of the cupcake and licked the leftover frosting from her fingers. She had almost got them completely clean and no longer needed the paper towel when Jewel burst in.

"Oh, my gosh. You'll never guess what I overheard."

"I'm sorry. I should have warned you that the men's room is right next door to the women's and the walls are a little too thin," Melody said.

"What?" Jewel at first looked confused, but then realizing what Melody meant, she said, "Yuck. No, not that. I overheard this girl talking on her cell phone around the corner down a dark hall."

"Okay. Who was it?"

"I think it was that Maggie girl. At least I heard her say, 'This is Maggie.'"

"So?"

"So she said she had her plan all figured out. She was going to get back at you and get her revenge. She said she was going to ruin everything for you."

"What are you talking about?"

"I heard her. I don't know who she was talking to but she said she was going to teach you a lesson and she had already started to put her scheme in motion."

"Are you sure she was talking about me? Did she say my name?"

"No, not exactly."

"Then what makes you think it was me? What *exactly* did she say?"

"She didn't say your name. She didn't say anyone's name. But I know she was talking about you."

"How? How do you know she was talking about me? How do you know she was talking about a person at all?"

Jewel scratched her head. "I don't, I guess. I just got the feeling she was talking about you." Pouting, she continued, "I just don't trust her."

Before Melody could question Jewel's obvious misplaced logic further, Maggie walked in. Jewel jumped and hugged her knees to your chest.

"I'm sorry," said Maggie, "I didn't mean to scare you."

"She's all right. She just came back from the ladies room," Melody said.

Maggie dramatically shook her head up and down. "That can be an unnerving experience the first time. After you've been here awhile, you get used to it, though."

"Jewel, this is Maggie, my colleague. Maggie, this is Jewel."

"Her best friend," Jewel interjected.

"Nice to meet you. I was stopping by to ask you if you want to go to the movies with us tonight. A few of us are going to see that new thriller with all of the murder, revenge, and betrayal you can handle. Jewel, you're welcome to come, too."

Melody said, "Thanks, but my parents are expecting me home for dinner."

"That's right. You're only sixteen. I keep forgetting."

"Thank you. Maybe some other time?"

"Sure," Maggie said. "Again, nice meeting you, Jewel. See you tomorrow, Melody."

Melody glared at Jewel as Maggie walked away. When she was sure Maggie was out of earshot, she scolded her. "You see, she was talking about a movie. Why do you always have to be so dramatic?" she said through clenched teeth.

Jewel shrugged. "I'm sorry. I guess I misunderstood."

"That's okay. No harm was done." Melody shut down her computer. "Let's get out of here," she said.

That night as Melody waited for sleep, after her giggles subsided from the memory of Jewel's misunderstanding about Maggie, she mentally rehearsed Candy's deposition in her mind. She would be asking the questions and another young attorney from the firm who didn't know anything about the case would be there to make sure she didn't make any big mistakes and correct them if she did. As hard as she tried, she couldn't put anyone other than Eric's face on the associate accompanying her at the deposition. She fell asleep to the screenplay of her and Eric as an efficient legal team.

She woke up with a feeling of longing. She looked at her clock, 3:02 a.m. She dreamt that Eric came into her office and closed the door behind him.

"There is something else I want that my parents don't want me to have, Melody," he said, taking her hands in his. Then he kneeled and he kissed her. She only felt his lips on hers for a moment before she woke up. She tried to go back to sleep and to where her dream had ended, but couldn't.

Eric did not work the rest of the week but it, like her dream, lingered. The day immediately after, Melody felt like Eric was there next to her. The connection she felt to him made her wonder if he was thinking about her as well. The days seemed to pass so slowly. She missed Eric and was anxious for the beginning of a new week so she could see him again. Early Friday afternoon, she received a text:

> Hi Melody,
> How's your week going? I talked to my parents and I'm still alive. Can't wait to fill you in on Monday.
> -Eric

Melody knew Eric's text made her feel happier than it should have. She deleted and re-wrote her reply for two hours before sending it:

Hey Eric,
My week is going soooooooo
sloooooooow. I'm glad you
talked to your parents...and
you are still breathing. I'll
look forward to Monday.
-Melody

She wanted to keep her reply simple and friendly, following Eric's format so as to not give too much away.

Melody feigned being tired from a busy week so she could hide away in her bedroom the entire weekend, listening to music and trying to figure out what to do about Eric. The battle within her raged. She obsessed over whether Eric thought of her just as a friend, had feelings for her, or if he even thought of her as a friend at all. She thought he must have or he wouldn't have sent her the text on Friday. Then she thought, *Eric is going to follow his rock and roll dream and I am going to be left here in the legal world.*

Eric had never said anything negative about his girlfriend, who served as a devoted fan of his band and helped them set up their equipment, so Melody knew she was not going anywhere. What baffled Melody the most was why she even cared at all. Eric would have no impact on her life in the long term and the odds were high that without the bond of the firm, their friendship would fade and die away. The only insights she gained from her secluded weekend of pondering was that she was afraid of losing Eric's friendship, but she still did not know why, and the best action would be to just be honest with Eric about her feelings. *Then*, she thought, *either I'll have confirmation of his friendship or I'll scare him away and won't have to worry about it anymore.*

Melody didn't come out of her room except for a little while on Sunday afternoon to play baseball with Marky and Justice in the back yard. After spending time with Marky, laughing and conversing about the things burning in a six-year-old's mind, she felt better and thought maybe adopting a policy of avoidance and denial by keeping busy would've been a better strategy than trying to think through the issues, which left her more confused and frustrated. Jewel called twice but Melody told her she wasn't feeling well enough to talk. She tried to call Jewel back, but the call went straight to voice mail. Figuring she'd let her phone's battery die, she called their home phone. Jordan answered and said she went to the mall with some friends from her school. The weekend ended as it began – in limbo.

Chapter Fourteen
The Deposition

"Mr. Harrison, how long have you owned the Midland Marquee Theater building?"

"Fifteen years next July." Ron Harrison answered Melody's questions succinctly. It was obvious to Melody that he'd had ample preparation with his attorney. He apparently was a good student, following the most stringent rules of being deposed: be brief, listen closely, and only answer the question. Candy was much chattier, so chatty at times she caught Candy's attorney staring her down. Melody could almost hear him saying, "Shut up, shut up," to Candy in his head.

"Mr. Harrison, you were here for Ms. Carstens' deposition, correct?"

"Yes."

"And you heard Ms. Carstens explain Dr. Maerow's office note was inaccurate and she actually told Dr. Maerow her ankle *felt* like a refrigerator had fallen on it the morning she fell at your antique store as opposed to feeling like she fell on stairs. Do you remember that?"

"Yes."

"Did Ms. Carstens mention anything to you about her ankle feeling like a refrigerator had fallen on it?"

"No, she did not."

"Did Ms. Carstens mention or even say the word 'refrigerator' at any time that day?"

"Not that I recall." Ron was not going to refute Candy's rationalization of Dr. Maerow's note. Melody knew her next step was to depose Dr. Maerow directly to authenticate his note and hopefully confirm that Ms. Carstens specifically said her refrigerator *fell* on her that morning and not that her ankle *felt* like a refrigerator had fallen on it.

Melody shifted her questions to another key area in the case: whether Ron Harrison had made reasonable efforts to ensure the property was maintained and in adequate repair.

"In your Answer, you denied stating to Ms. Carstens you had recently fallen on the very stairs upon which she fell. Do you still deny making that statement?"

"Yes," said Ron.

"In the documents submitted in Candy's slip and fall case, you indicated you were not aware the stairs in your building were hazardous and you made every effort to keep apprised of the building's condition, maintain it, and make any repairs necessary to preserve the safety of your patrons so, therefore, you are not legally liable for Ms. Carstens' injuries. Is that an accurate statement?"

"Yes, I believe it is."

"In your response to our Request for Production of Documents, you asserted you had no documents, notes, or other written materials reflecting the repairs and maintenance you've performed or have performed on the building. Since that time, have you located any such documents?"

"No." Ron leaned back in his chair, rested his right foot on his left knee, and rubbed his chin. Melody got the feeling that Ron was not too sure about his answer.

"So you don't have any receipts, quotes, work orders, brochures, or anything like that?" Melody pressed.

Ron hesitated, still rubbing his chin. He dropped his right foot to the floor with a thump and then sat up straight, leaning his forearms on the table. He closed his right eye and squinted the left, as if he was digging somewhere deep in his mind.

"You know what?" Ron slapped his right hand on the top of the table. The platter holding coffee cups and creamer packets clattered. "The basement at the store is plumb full of old papers. There are papers down there, I believe, from pretty near when it was built. It's where I store all my papers, too."

"Do you know if there are any receipts or anything that might reference any maintenance or repairs?"

"You know, there might be. I save everything, so I'd think there'd be stuff down there about repairs."

"Okay. Then I would ask you to provide any documents referencing any work on the building to your attorney and supplement your responses to our discovery requests."

Ron shook his head, "There are just stacks and stacks of boxes down there. I'd have to look through them all to find what you want."

"Well, the repairs and maintenance of the building are important, so we need them."

"I'm sorry, but I can't do that." Melody didn't know how to respond. Up to that point, the depositions were friendly. She was not prepared for an argument. She looked at Ron's attorney for help in convincing his client to provide the needed documents, but he was looking out the window, a slight smile curling just half of his mouth. Melody was about to reiterate how important the documents were when the associate from her office sent to assist her, Jackson, spoke up.

"Mr. Siefert, we're going to have to insist on getting any documents about any work done on the building from those boxes. They speak directly to the issues in this case."

Gary Siefert turned his attention from the window to the table, tilted his head up slightly, and peered at Melody over the top rims of his glasses. "Mr. Harrison doesn't have the time to go through all of the documents and asking him to do so would be overly burdensome. I think, however, we can make them available to you if you want to come over and look through them." Gary turned his head to Ron.

"Oh, yes, yes, that's fine. You can come over whenever you like. Just give me a call," said Ron, nodding his head in affirmation. "You might want to bring him," Ron said, pointing at Jackson, "or someone else because there is an awful lot of heavy boxes down there." Melody immediately thought of Eric and picturing them toiling away over boxes of documents caused her heart to jolt.

"They can't call you, Ron, but Melody here will call me and we'll call you to set up a time." Gary again stared at Melody over the rims of his bifocals. He said, "Sound okay? Do you want to call tomorrow?"

Melody regained her senses, "Yes, I will. Should I speak directly with you, Mr. Siefert?"

"No, ask for my secretary and she'll set you up."

The rest of the deposition finished without Melody extracting any more information. When she got back to her office, she began typing her notes into a report to e-mail to Dan. She was so engrossed in her typing, her eyes glazed over, watching the words form on her computer screen. She heard a soft knock on her doorjamb and looked up to find Eric leaning into the doorway, smiling.

"You're back?"

"Yeah, about a half hour ago. I'm typing up my notes for your dad."

Eric sat down in the chair across from Melody's desk. "So tell me everything. How did it go? Were you nervous?"

"I was nervous at first but it was just like sitting down for a conversation, so I was fine after a few minutes."

"What did Candy have to say about that medical record?"

"That reminds me, I need to call the doctor's office to schedule his deposition." Melody wrote a note on a piece of yellow sticky paper and stuck it on her computer monitor. "Candy claims she told the doctor her foot *felt* like a refrigerator fell on her ankle."

"Wow, she's quick on her feet anyway."

"Yeah. So now I need to get the doctor deposed and hopefully he'll say he remembered Candy saying what he wrote in his note or at least say he makes such accurate records, and he's sure that the statement is correct."

"That sounds good. Is there anything else I can help you with?" Eric began to push himself up by grabbing both chair arms.

"Actually there is." Eric sat back down. "Apparently, Mr. Harrison has boxes and boxes of documents in the theater's basement he 'forgot' about until today," said Melody, making air quotes with her fingers. "So I'm going to have to go over there to go through all of these boxes to see what repair receipts I can find."

"I can do that. When can I go?"

"Evidently, there are so many boxes it is more than a one person job so I was thinking if we both went, maybe we could get it done in a day."

"I see. So you need a strapping young lad to protect you from the basement rodents, do you?" Eric joked, flexing his biceps.

"Right, more like just scare them away with your face. Ha, ha, take that," said Melody.

"Oh, really?" Eric folded his arms across his chest, pretending to pout. "Maybe you can just put up a picture of me down there then."

"Maybe, but the boxes are so heavy, I need someone to help me shuffle them around. I don't want to break a nail." She waved her fingers at Eric.

Eric took her hand and held his fingers toward his face, "Looks like someone already took care of your nails. Or maybe you mean you don't want to break your nubs?"

Melody laughed and snapped her hand back. "Are you going to help me or not?"

Eric stood up, took an invisible hat off his head, swung it in front of his body, and bowed, "I'd be delighted to, little miss. Just tell me the day and time." Melody giggled and shook her head.

"It will be sometime next week. I have to call to set it up. Are you here every afternoon next week?"

"I will be here Monday through Wednesday next week until five. Thursday is Thanksgiving and Friday is Amy's and my second anniversary so I won't be in."

"I forgot about Thanksgiving," said Melody. "I'll try for the beginning of the week after that then."

Eric said, "Okay," and walked out. After he left, she thought she should've congratulated Eric on his anniversary and made a mental note to do so next week.

Before leaving for the day, Melody called Dr. Maerow's office. She talked to his secretary and, to her surprise, got several dates when Dr. Maerow could give his deposition within the next month. She was grateful the doctor's schedule was so flexible. She knew if they could get the testimony they wanted from him, they might be able to derail Candy's case against Ron Harrison, which would mean preserving the Midland Marquee Theater and minimizing MPOPS' fees. Accomplishing that would help Melody to build credibility as an attorney in the firm and in the community.

The next day, Eric wasn't at work. Melody scheduled their visit to the theater's basement for a week from Tuesday and when she went to tell him, the conference room where he usually worked was dark. She looked in some of the other places Eric liked to work, the back library table with walls to disguise him if he thought he might doze off or, since Dan was gone, his father's office, resting his feet on Dan's desk in defiance. He hadn't mentioned not being in and Melody worried he may be ill. She asked the receptionist, "Do you know if Eric is in today?"

"No, he called and said his band got hired to play at a birthday party at the last minute."

"Okay, thanks." Melody hoped the receptionist couldn't detect her disappointment; disappointment not only about not getting to see Eric that day, but because he didn't call her to tell her about his band's engagement.

She couldn't concentrate for the rest of the afternoon. She kept playing her most recent conversation with Eric over in her head, trying to meticulously replay every word and every deflection in every syllable to find a hint about his feelings. On the one hand, he was so friendly and he took her hand, but then he brought up his anniversary with his girlfriend. Melody knew she was missing Eric more than she was entitled. She felt silly and torn up inside. She couldn't go on like this much longer. She felt like she was deceiving him by pretending to be his friend but secretly having these feelings well beyond those of friendship.

Chapter Fifteen
The Hunt

On the Tuesday following Thanksgiving, Melody and Eric spent the afternoon at the Midland Marque Theater's basement. The boxes were full of dust. Each time they lifted the lid off one of the banker's boxes, a puff of dust spurted out and Melody sneezed. She sorted through the documents, attempting to discreetly sniff her runny nose. Not only did the dust irritate her, but it was the end of November, the weather was chilly, and the old basement was even colder. Every time Melody thought she was getting better, she was done looking through her box and had to get out another. Eric arrived more prepared than Melody, dressed in loose blue jeans and a sweat shirt. At first, she was taken aback by his appearance and thought how cute he looked in his more casual attire and a baseball cap taming his curls. Melody wore her usual business suit and low-heeled flats. She was uncomfortable in her dress clothes and bulky black wool coat. Halfway through the afternoon, she pictured how she must look in her professional clothes with random streaks of dust covering them and her hair a mess, rifling through boxes in a dank dark basement and she laughed out loud.

"What's so funny?" Eric asked, startled, looking up from a manila folder. His sudden movement made the dust falling to the floor in the tiny stream of sunlight cutting across the room look like snow.

"I was just thinking about how we must look, wondering if we're on one of those practical-joke reality TV shows."

Eric laughed. "I must look like someone who's been wallowing in the dirt all day."

"Well, yes, but I was thinking more about how I must look."

"No way. You look divine, like you're headed to the ball."

"Thank you for being such a good liar," Melody said in the most dramatic and condescending tone she could muster. She smiled at Eric and he held her gaze long enough to cause Melody's face to flush. She turned her head quickly back to the box in front of her, acting deeply engrossed in it. She was grateful that the basement was so dark and he couldn't see her blushing.

By late in the afternoon, they had gone through most of the documents and found a lot of marginally interesting papers, but no receipts or anything referring to the building's maintenance or repair. The sunlight streaming in through the basement's tiny windows became more horizontal, dimming as it crawled up the wall on the opposite side of the room.

Eric looked at his watch. "It's four-thirty. Can we call it quits yet?"

"We only have those boxes left to look through." Melody pointed to a stack of discolored boxes lined up and stacked four wide and three deep along the back wall. "Since we've found nothing so far, I think the likelihood of finding anything useful in those is minimal but, what if they are just full of receipts and we don't know?" She stood with her hands on her hips and bit her lower lip. She tucked a loose lock of hair behind her ear, massaged the back of her neck, and turned to Eric, "What do you think?"

"I think you're right. Isn't that Murphy's law where what you need is in the very last place you look?"

"Technically it's what can go wrong will, but that's close. Maybe we could just take a quick shuffle through them and then decide where to go from there?"

Eric agreed, "You start on that end and I'll start on this end."

Melody lifted the top box off the stack. The bottom of the box gave way, and the contents dropped on her feet. Eric tried to rescue her, but couldn't get to her in time. He took the box from her hands just as the last piece of paper fell. He was left holding an empty box with the wilted bottom dangling in shreds. He looked at Melody's buried feet and began laughing hysterically. Melody laughed and crouched down to begin gathering up the scattered papers and file folders.

Eric continued to laugh and then he started to cough. He choked out, "I'm sorry, are you okay? You looked so bewildered and in shock and I couldn't help myself."

Melody stood and patted him on the back, "I'm glad I could entertain you. Except for the paper cuts severing my foot, I'm okay."

Eric's hacking calmed.

"Maybe we should both start at this end?"

"Good idea," Melody agreed. They gathered the fallen papers and stacked them in the overturned lid of a box she had already reviewed and continued ruffling through the remaining boxes, being careful to support the bottoms as they lifted them. She considered quitting about halfway through when they still hadn't found anything, but she thought they'd better not, just in case. By the time they got through the last box and stacked them all as they had found them, the dim sunlight had vanished. The only light was a bare bulb in the middle of the room.

Thinking she saw a shadow in the window out of the corner of her eye, Melody jumped. "What was that?"

"What was what?"

"I thought I saw a shadow outside the window."

Eric stood on an upside down empty crate and looked out. He wiped the thick dust from it with the back of his hand. "I don't see anything."

"It must be my imagination. Let's hurry."

After Eric pushed the last box in line with the one under it, he said, "Wow, this has been fun. Let's do it again real soon."

"Let's get out of here. The shadows from that light are making it even creepier down here and my mind keeps playing tricks on me, making me think I keep seeing that same shadow in the window."

"Oooh, is brainy Melody afraid of the boogey-man?" Eric mocked her, lifted his arm, and curled his fingers toward her like a monster. He stepped back and the string hanging down from the light fixture brushed his left ear. He jumped, releasing a guttural terrified groan and violently swiped his ear, "What the..."

Melody immediately doubled over in laughter. Eric swung around and saw the string that attacked him. He whipped the string downward. The room turned black and the metal chain tinkled lightly against the light bulb's thin glass. He took Melody's hand and pulled her up the stairs and out of the basement. He kept her hand in his until they exited the building, locking the door behind them. They stood facing each other in the glow of the nearby street light.

"That was....interesting," said Melody.

"Yeah, it was." Eric took off his cap and pushed his hair back. Replacing it, he said, "It was kind of fun, though."

"We had some laughs, that's for sure."

"I have to say I can't think of a better person to spend an entire afternoon with in a dirty, cold basement than you." Eric smiled softly. He didn't look away. Melody dropped her head to examine her toes. She slowly lifted her head. He was still looking at her and she didn't look away.

Her heart thumped hard in her chest and she thought Eric was about to kiss her when he broke the silence, "You're such a good friend, Melody. I've really liked working with you. And not just today. With you around, pretending to be a future lawyer is actually bearable."

"Thanks." Melody pointed over her shoulder to her car parked behind her on the street. "Well, I'd better be going."

"Okay. See you tomorrow." Eric lightly touched Melody's shoulder as she turned to go to her car. She looked back and gave a half wave before burying her hands in her pockets. Eric held his hand in a traffic officer's stop-gesture in response.

As she drove home, Melody's head swam with conflicting thoughts and emotions. She was confused at Eric's behavior in contrast with his statement about being such a good friend, but she was glad that he had confirmed he indeed thought of her as his friend.

When Melody walked in the front door, she found her dad alone in the living room. He folded down his paper, lifted it back up, and then did a double take. "What happened to you?"

"Don't ask. It was a long day, Dad, involving a lot of dust and old paperwork."

"I guess." Max pointed to the kitchen. "I think Mom left you a plate of dinner in the fridge."

"I'm not really hungry. I feel kind of sick from the dust, I think. I'm just going to take a shower and head to bed." She suddenly noticed the silence of the house. "Where's Mom and Marky?"

"They had to run out to the store to get a gift for the birthday party Marky is going to on Saturday."

"Tell Mom I said thanks for making me a plate. And I'll leave you to your rare time of peace."

"Thanks, honey." Max chuckled. She was already halfway down the hall to her bedroom when he called out, "Anyone ever tell you you're one smart cookie?"

"Ha, ha, Dad. Goodnight!"

She was just about to doze off when she was startled by her cell phone screaming in her purse, which was hanging across the room on her door knob. She jumped up and rushed to answer it before it woke up everyone in the house. After fumbling through her purse for what seemed like an eternity trying to find her phone, she realized she needn't have worried because it was only nine o'clock.

"Hello."

"Hey, Mel. How's it going?"

"Hi, Jewel. Okay, I guess. What's up with you?" She was actually relieved Jewel had woke her up with her phone call. She thought maybe it was a sign telling her that she should tell Jewel about her Eric dilemma and ask for some advice.

"Oh, Melody, life is so awesome. I think I'm in love."

"Really? That's great!" Melody said, then remembering how her feelings for Eric were tearing her up inside, threw in, "Isn't it?"

"Of course it's great! Chad is so wonderful." For the next half an hour Jewel relayed every detail of every contact she'd had with Chad in the last two weeks. Melody was so exhausted from work and worry she hadn't talked to Jewel more than a minute or two at a time in those two weeks. She thought she should make a better effort to spend more time with Jewel so she could get the "all about Chad show" in several increments rather than one epic session.

"Wow, I missed this, Mel. It seems like we haven't talked in forever."

"I know, Jewel. I'm sorry. I've just been so exhausted from working that I don't have much energy lately. Tonight I was in bed by eight."

"Uh oh. It sounds like you're getting old. I think those old stuffy lawyers are rubbing off on you."

Melody laughed halfheartedly. "Maybe, but it's almost ten and I need to go back tomorrow, so I've got to get some sleep." She no longer had the energy to bring up Eric and spend another hour on the phone.

"Okay. I'll let you get back to your beauty sleep, but we have to make some plans to get together," said Jewel. "What are you doing Saturday?"

Melody hesitated slightly, fearful of Jewel's reaction. "I have plans with Maggie on Saturday." She cringed and was surprised by Jewel's level response.

"All right. Maybe some other time."

But she could tell Jewel was hiding her true feelings. "I'm sorry, Jewel. There's a bar association carnival for lawyers who graduated from law school less than ten years ago."

"Bar association? But you're lawyers. What does that have to do with a bar?"

"It's just the name of the professional organization for attorneys. It's named after the 'bar exam' you take to get your license, but I don't remember why they call it 'the bar' either." Melody struggled to remember what she was saying before being interrupted by Jewel's inquisitiveness. "Anyway, Maggie asked me to go with her a month ago when it was first announced. She said she'd introduce me to some people; help me do some networking."

"Help you do some networking?" Jewel sounded suspicious.

142

"She said it's always good to meet people from other firms, just in case."

"In case of what?" The suspicion in Jewel's voice was unmistakable now. She had talked about being a detective one day, and it seemed to Melody she had a natural talent for the profession.

"I don't know, Jewel. In case I have to work opposite with them on a lawsuit, I assume. They'd be more likely to be agreeable if they know me personally."

"Or is it in case you find yourself in need of employment?"

"I don't know. That's just what she said." Melody was getting annoyed. "I'm really tired. What are you doing the rest of the weekend?"

"I'm going out with Chad Friday and Saturday nights but I'm free Sunday."

"Sunday I promised my parents I'd spend the day with Marky so they can have a date-day."

"Fine."

"I'm sorry, Jewel. Maybe the next weekend."

"Yeah, whatever."

Melody felt terrible when Jewel was angry with her and she tried to smooth over the situation. "I'm really sorry and I really don't want to go to this thing with Maggie, but she asked me a month ago."

"Why didn't you mention it that day I was in the office?"

"I didn't think of it. I already said I would go, plus it's never a bad idea to network."

"I said it's fine." Melody could tell it was definitely not fine, but was sorry she pressed for more information. When she did, Jewel's anger blew through Melody's phone speaker though she tried her hardest to conceal it with care and concern. "I don't trust this Maggie person. She's so much older than you and it sounds like she is popular enough, so I don't understand why she wants to hang out with you so much."

"I think she doesn't want to hang out with me as a friend her own age but more as a big sister. She's just being nice and maybe she's trying to be a mentor, but that's not a crime."

"Well, I still think she's plotting against you. And what does she mean by 'just in case'?"

"One day, we'll all have to do something together, and you will see she is just being nice."

"If you're not going to listen to me, then you're on your own." Melody no longer had the energy to try to calm Jewel. They exchanged brisk goodbyes before hanging up.

Melody lay down face up in her bed. She pulled her blankets to her neck and closed her eyes. She tried to sleep, but Jewel's anger rang in her ears and Eric's face felt as if it was permanently painted on the inside of her eyelids.

Why is everything such a disaster? she thought, feeling angry, hurt, and like she had no one to turn to. A tear slipped out of the corner of her eye, slid down her cheek, and into her ear. She rubbed it and muttered, "I can't even cry right," grabbing her blanket and yanking it over her head, exposing her feet. She ripped off the covers and threw them. Justice whined and then scurried out of her room, his head hanging toward the hardwood floor. She swung to a sitting position on the edge of her bed and dropped her feet.

She bent over, put her elbows on her knees, and rested her forehead in her hands. She looked at her toes and tried to concentrate on the silence beyond her own voice berating her in her head. She felt and heard a low grumble in her stomach and thought, *If I'm not going to sleep, I might as well eat.*

Melody tip-toed to the kitchen. It was after ten-thirty now and she didn't want to wake her parents or Marky. She found the plate of dinner her mother had left for her in the refrigerator and heated it in the microwave, careful to open the door before the timer expired and set off the piercing microwave alarms.

She ate listlessly, propping up her head with her hand, her elbow on the table. She was relieved that she was alone and no one was there to correct her poor table manners. She took a bite and then gingerly sat her fork in her plate while she chewed, considering her options and imagining the consequences of each one. Her tears ebbed and flowed. She did not bother to wipe them away or care if they were saturating and salting her food.

I can't keep living like this, she thought, *I have to do something*. She forced herself to be completely honest with herself. She admitted she had romantic feelings for Eric and she might even be in love with him. She also admitted to herself that there could be no future for her and Eric. Besides the fact he had not overtly expressed any interest in her besides friendship, their lives were headed in opposite directions and he had a girlfriend who he seemed very happy with.

Melody brought another bite of mashed potatoes to her lips. They tasted cold and rubbery after sitting so long. She dropped her fork onto her plate, shot up straight in the kitchen chair, and whispered loud, "I know what I have to do." She held her breath and looked around to make sure she hadn't attracted an investigation from her family. Everything was still silent. She scraped the rest of her food into the trash and placed her dishes into the sink. She leaned on the edge of the counter, looked out the window into the night, and thought, *I have to tell Eric the truth. I know it will probably scare him away and he won't want anything to do with me, but once he's gone, I can forget about him and move on.*

She turned the lights off as she returned to her room. She re-arranged her blankets on her bed and crawled in, pushing her feet under Justice, who had nested himself in the middle. She fell right to sleep, her mind more at ease now that a decision had been made.

Chapter Sixteen
The Confession

On Friday morning, Melody was greeted by her office telephone flashing to alert to her she had a voice mail message. She had never had one before and had to dig in her desk to find the instructions to retrieve it. It was Dr. Maerow's office confirming his deposition for the following Tuesday morning. Everything accelerated after Melody found out that the court had a criminal case it needed to schedule for the time slot Carstens v. Harrison was supposed to be in trial.

The court administrator responsible for the judge's schedule had called the day before to finalize the trial starting date. "I'm just calling to confirm the message left by someone in your office saying it was okay to move the date earlier."

This was the first Melody had heard of the change; Dan hadn't mentioned it to her. "Do you know who left the message?"

"No dear," the court administrator said, "It just says here that someone from Lazlo, Marshdon and Brown said it was fine to move the date up."

Assuming Dan approved the schedule change, Melody said, "Yes, that's fine. We will be ready eleven days from today." It made sense that the trial schedule had been quickened. Of course, Candy was anxious to see if she'd get her million dollars and Mr. Harrison wanted to know if he could schedule a demolition crew, so they were more than willing to move up the trial. The Midland Preserve Our Past Society wanted more time to try to find evidence that would save the theater, but after the fruitless basement investigation, it was not optimistic, so they must've agreed to get the trial out of the way so they could move on to other projects.

The only possibility Lazlo, Marshdon and Brown had to save the theater for MPOPS was Dr. Maerow's medical record exposing Candy's fraudulent injury. Dr. Maerow's testimony confirming his note as written was paramount to the case, so, if she was able to do nothing else to prepare for the trial, she needed the doctor's deposition.

Melody returned Dr. Maerow's office's phone call and then instructed Dan's administrative assistant, Angie, to prepare the Subpoena Duces Tecum Dr. Maerow required so he would know when and where to arrive for the deposition and the documents he needed to bring. For this deposition, Melody wanted Dr. Maerow to bring his original medical chart for Candy; many of the local doctors had digitized their records and could simply email them, but Dr. Maerow came from the paper generation and, as an independent doctor working by himself, he hadn't changed his record-keeping practices. She also asked Angie to draft a notice to send to Candy's and Ron's attorneys to provide the same information about the deposition's logistics and let them know about the subpoena she was sending to Dr. Maerow.

Melody hung up, turned on her computer, and remembered today was the day she'd decided to talk to Eric about her feelings. The attorneys in the office were attending a seminar and, with their bosses away, most of the administrative assistants planned to take the afternoon off. Melody thought the lack of curious eyes and ears might make things a little easier. She knew Eric was leaving by four so she planned to find him and talk to him at three.

The day wore slowly and the seconds seemed to pass like hours. Melody couldn't concentrate. Several times she had to force herself to breathe deep because she found her heart pounding so hard that she was holding in her breath. At one point, she began to see sparkles in front of her eyes and had to lay her head down. She wasn't hungry for lunch and felt somewhat nauseated so she spent her hour break with her door closed, making notes, and deciding exactly how she was going to break her news to Eric.

Finally, like in slow motion, the clock on Melody's computer changed to 3:00; she thought she could actually see the pixels on her computer monitor dimming and then lighting to change the formation from 2:59. She stood up, sucked in a deep breath, slowly pushed her chair under her desk, and walked deliberately to the conference room where Eric was working. She tried to stay calm and was surprised she was able to squeak out a "hello" to one of the few staff who did not leave early for the day.

Eric had his head in his palm, leaning his elbow on the table, when Melody knocked softly on the door jamb. "Hey, Melody, how's it going?" he said. She hoped he could not sense the sickening feeling in the pit of her stomach. Her heart pounded so hard in her ears, when she spoke it sounded like she was wearing ear plugs.

"I'm okay. How are you?" Melody asked, glancing at her reflection in the glass protecting the framed artwork on the conference room wall to see if her face was as ghostly as she feared.

"I'm good. Glad it's Friday, though." Eric smiled. "Is there something you need me to work on before I leave?"

"No, actually I was hoping to talk to you about something not work-related."

"Sure. Sit down." He gave no hint of suspecting what she was about to say.

She was as honest as she could be, "I'm kind of nervous about what I'm going to tell you, so if you'd just let me finish and then you can ask me any questions or whatever, okay?"

"Sure. Is everything okay?"

"Not really, well, sort of." Melody looked up to Eric's eyes and then feeling the urge to flee, she looked down at her hands fidgeting in her lap. She picked at her fingernails and explained, "You have been a good friend to me but I haven't been a very good friend to you." Eric made a noise like he was going to say something, but didn't.

"I have not been a very good friend to you because even though I act like your friend, I don't feel like just your friend. My feelings for you are way more than what I should have for a friend." With the worst of it out, Melody took a deep breath and continued, "I completely understand if you don't want to have anything to do with me now and I feel terrible about feeling this way, but it's not going away, so I thought I should be honest with you and let you decide what to do." Melody knew she was rambling, so she clasped her hands tightly and held her breath, waiting for Eric's response.

"Is it okay for me to respond now?" he asked. Melody shook her head up and down slightly, clenching her teeth in an attempt to stop the tears she could feel forming in the corners of her eyes.

"Thank you for your honesty, Melody. It's sweet of you to feel that way about me and I don't want us to stop being friends. I like working with you; you're fun to spend time with. And I hope you'll come see my band play sometime."

Melody felt relieved and confused at the same time. She said, "Thanks, Eric. I felt like such a fraud, like I was deceiving you somehow. I thought if we are friends I should just let you know and if you didn't want to be friends anymore, I'd respect that decision."

"I understand and I appreciate that. But everything is fine. We're still friends, okay?"

Still feeling uncomfortable, Melody agreed and then excused herself to write a letter she said she had forgotten about that needed to be sent before she left for the day. She nearly ran back to her office. She closed the door, sat down, laid her head on her desk, and let the tears form tiny pools, distorting the painted wood grain in the desk's laminate top. *What did you think would happen?* Melody asked herself, but she wasn't sure. She didn't know if she thought or hoped Eric would say he had feelings for her, too. She just knew what she thought would happen, that he would say he couldn't be friends with her any longer, didn't happen and she had no idea what to do next.

Chapter Seventeen
Bar Association Carnival

The alarm clock startled Melody from a deep sleep.

She groaned. "Ugh, it's Saturday." Then she remembered Maggie was picking her up at nine for the bar association carnival. Ever since leaving work yesterday, she had begun to feel more and more embarrassed about telling Eric about her feelings. Remembering that, she flopped back onto her bed, slapping her forehead with both hands.

"Ow. Great, now I'll probably have handprints on my forehead," she said out loud. Justice, curled deep in sleep at the end of her bed, lifted his head. She thought she saw him roll his eyes before dropping back down into his paws. She showered and thought about how much she did not feel like spending the day with Maggie, meeting new people, and forcing polite conversation.

Maggie arrived at exactly nine. Melody heard the door bell ring and came around the corner as Marky, still in his pajamas, opened the door. Meredith came up behind him. She grabbed his shoulders and turned him to face her, "Marky, what is the rule about opening the door when someone rings the doorbell or knocks?"

Marky looked toward the ceiling, putting his index finger to his lips. He squinted and said, "Ask who it is?"

"That's right. And if you don't know the person, what do you do?"

"Get you or Daddy?"

"Right. Now try harder to remember next time, okay?" Marky shook his head in agreement and then ran away up to his room. Meredith stood and held her hand out to Maggie. "Hi, I'm Melody's mom, Meredith. Come on in." Pointing to the imaginary cloud of dust Marky left, she said, "And that little crazy boy who answered the door was her brother, Mark."

Melody, finding her balance after nearly being knocked over, walked down the stairs just as Meredith was about to call out to her.

"Hi Maggie. Did you have any problem finding the house?" said Melody.

"Nope. Your directions were great. Are you ready?"

Melody plucked her jacket off the hall tree next to the door and followed Maggie to her car, a red convertible Mustang with the top down. Even though it was warmer than usual, it was still December and too chilly to have the top down. Melody opened the passenger door and carefully slid onto the cream-colored leather seat. She was glad Maggie seemed not to hear the embarrassing noise she made as did.

"Isn't this weather great?" said Maggie, plopping into the driver's seat. "I love the fresh cool air in my hair, don't you?"

Melody didn't know how to answer.

"I'm originally from northern Minnesota," Maggie explained. "By this time of year, there is usually at least a foot of snow on the ground already."

"I see," Melody said, but thought the weather that day was too cold to have the top down even if she was used to North Pole weather.

Melody barely had her seatbelt clicked when Maggie slammed on her accelerator and squealed onto the street. Melody zipped her jacket up as high as she could, wishing she'd grabbed something heavier.

"Your little brother is cute. How old is he?" Maggie yelled, but Melody still had to lean closer to hear her question. The wind roaring around the windshield and her hair whipping her ears was loud.

"He's six. Marky's great. He's a lot of fun," Melody yelled back. She gathered her hair back into a ponytail with her frozen hand to keep it from blowing in her watering eyes. She was grateful Maggie didn't ask her any more questions. She kept silent so Maggie could concentrate on her driving and so she could conserve her energy to retain body heat.

When they arrived at the building housing the carnival, the parking lot was empty and Melody wondered if they were at the right location.

Maggie said, "I guess we're early." She looked at her watch. "We're not that early. I must have missed class the day they taught lawyers how to never be on time."

"Me, too."

"I really don't want to be the first ones there. Do you want to walk over there and get a coffee?" asked Maggie.

"Sounds great. I need a coffee. I'm not used to being awake this early on a Saturday." *And maybe it will thaw me out*, Melody added in her head.

"Maybe that's the problem. They should start this thing in the afternoon."

Melody thought perhaps her theory about having fun being directly proportional to how much she *didn't* look forward to something was going to be proven again. After her frozen car ride, she hadn't been so sure. Maggie and Melody got their coffees and, seeing the parking lot only slightly less empty than when they left, strolled slowly. Melody embraced her steaming cup with both hands and held it close to her body to absorb the heat.

"So how is your case with Dan going? I heard the trial got moved way up."

"It did. It starts a week from Monday."

"Are you ready for it?"

"I think so. I have a deposition on Tuesday and then just have to get ready for the actual trial."

"Who's getting deposed?"

"The plaintiff's doctor."

"Is he important?"

"He might end up being our key witness. He's the one that made the note I told you about."

"What was that again?" Maggie took a sip of her coffee and looked behind them. Melody thought she was being cautious, ensuring she was aware of her surroundings like they teach in self-defense class.

"Well, I don't know what you remember, but the plaintiff, Candy, claims she fell in the antique shop our clients are trying to save from demolition, but Dr. Maerow has a note in his chart saying otherwise."

Maggie was acutely interested, which Melody attributed to a mutual appreciation of the law and litigation. "Oh yes. I think I remember. Didn't it say something about a refrigerator?" Maggie asked.

"The note says Candy told her doctor that the morning before she went to the antique shop, she was moving her refrigerator in her house and it fell on her ankle."

"That's right. So you just need the doctor to authenticate the record, to confirm it is his record?" Melody ignored the unnecessary explanation for the definition of "authenticate." People sometimes forgot that although she was only sixteen, Melody was as knowledgeable, if not more so, than people twice her age. She knew that they meant no disrespect, so she always tried to disregard what sometimes felt like belittling.

"Actually, we need more than that from Dr. Maerow. Candy claimed at her deposition she told him after she fell on the stairs, her ankle *felt* like a refrigerator had fallen on it and Dr. Maerow's note is incorrect…"

"So you need the doctor to remember the plaintiff saying the refrigerator fell on her." Maggie finished.

"Right. That's the ideal. We'll also take him saying he always takes accurate notes and if he wrote it in his note, Candy said it, even if he doesn't remember it independently."

Maggie suddenly stopped mid-stride and grabbed Melody's right forearm. The heat from her coffee radiated from her hand through her light jacket. Maggie said, "This is Dr. Maerow's office isn't it?"

"Yes."

"I worked on a case involving a patient from his office before. He's all paper. So I hope you have that record in a safe place."

Melody thought Maggie was being a bit over-dramatic. "It's in with the other binders of records in the conference room where we've been working."

"A lot of times, we'll put really important documents like that in the firm's safe, just in case."

"I never thought of that. I'll have to check into it on Monday." But she didn't intend to put the record under lock and key. It was just a copy and they could always get another from the doctor's office if they needed to.

By the time they arrived back at the carnival, they had finished their coffees and several cars were parked in the lot. They threw their empty cups into the trash container next to the door before going in. After registering, Maggie began introducing Melody to the other young attorneys.

The auditorium in the building was set up like a carnival with different games to play. There was good food and several flavors of soda. Local vendors with products young lawyers might be interested in like briefcases, cell phones, and voice recording equipment also attended. Melody quickly became the main attraction. It seemed like everyone wanted to meet and talk to her. She enjoyed the attention; it was nice to have people she actually had something in common with be so interested in her.

Melody was so busy telling everyone her story of skipping grades in school, how she got interested in law, and became a lawyer, that she didn't notice Maggie was no longer with the circle of new friends surrounding her. Once she realized this, she pushed herself to her toes and tried to look over the taller crowd to find her. Between shoulders, she finally spotted Maggie leaning against the wall, her arms crossed over her chest, a cup of soda to her lips.

Melody thought Maggie looked bored and she felt bad for abandoning her after she was so nice to bring her to the carnival. As she got closer, Melody thought she looked more annoyed than bored, but when Maggie spotted her out of the corner of her eye, she smiled brightly.

"Hey, Miss Popularity, are you having fun?"

"Yes, I am. Thanks for inviting me here. I'm sorry, I got sidetracked talking to everyone and lost track of you."

If Maggie was annoyed, she seemed to forgive her. "No problem. I brought you to help you network and you seem to be doing great at it." Maggie waved Melody away. "I'll be fine. Go, have fun."

"That's okay. I guess I didn't know I'd be the side show." Maggie laughed and Melody asked, "Want to do the ring toss with me? Looks like we could win a bar association key ring."

Maggie took the last drink of her soda and tossed her cup into a nearby trashcan. "Sure. One can never have enough bar association promotional junk."

Melody enjoyed the rest of the afternoon with Maggie. They played the ring toss game, threw softballs at wood milk bottles, and picked rubber ducks out of a plastic child's pool. They each went home with key chains, water bottles, and beach towels embossed with the bar association logo. Melody put her prizes in her new hot pink briefcase that cost more than she should have spent, but it was so cool she couldn't resist.

She spent the rest of the weekend feeling more hopeful about being a lawyer and her place in the world. She thought maybe she just might be able to find some normalcy in the legal world after all. Though the other attorneys at the bar association event were curious and had a lot of questions, they really just seemed interested in her as a colleague and not as the freak show attraction she usually felt like. For the first time in a long time, Melody fell asleep Sunday night in peace. She was ready to take on the busy week that lay ahead.

Chapter Eighteen
Vanished

The office phone rang, startling Melody. Hot coffee splashed when she jumped, burning her upper lip. It was mid-morning on Monday and she was going over her outline of questions for Dr. Maerow's deposition. All she could hear when she answered the phone was a faint scratching noise in the distance. She thought whoever was calling had intended to call someone else, which happened often because everyone's phone numbers were sequential and it was easy to push the wrong digit.

"Hello. This is Melody." Still no response except for the distant scratching. "Hello. Can I help you?"

"Yes, I'm sorry."

She waited. "May I ask who's calling?"

"I apologize. This is Nancy from Dr. Maerow's office. We have to cancel Doctor's deposition tomorrow."

"Okay. When can we reschedule?"

"We can't reschedule."

"The trial is Monday."

"He's not going to be available."

Melody was becoming frustrated and tried to change Nancy's mind. "But I really need to depose him. His testimony is key to the case. May I please speak with him?"

"No, you can't." There was a long moment of silence and then what sounded like a muffled horn on Nancy's end of the line. "Dr. Maerow is gone."

"Excuse me? Did you say Dr. Maerow is…?"

"Gone. Yes."

"I'm so sorry. How did it happen?"

"He just closed up and took off."

Melody was confused by Nancy's unusual metaphor for death. "Was it a heart attack?"

"No, more like a mid-life crisis, we think."

"How does someone die from a mid-life crisis?"

"Oh no, he's not dead."

"But you said he was…"

"Yeah, he's gone. He left. He ran away." Nancy explained they opened the office that morning to find a letter from Dr. Maerow saying he was leaving the practice and closing it. He said they wouldn't be able to find him because he was not taking a cell phone and there were no other means of getting in touch with him.

"He said he just wanted to get lost and forget about everything in his past life." Nancy's tears resumed.

"That's terrible. His poor family."

"We called his wife and she said he left her a similar note."

"Did she call the police?"

"I asked her that. She snapped at me and said the police won't look for a grown man who ran away from home."

"Did you ask her if she had any idea of where he might go?"

"I did. She said she didn't have any ideas and, besides, he only took $10,000 from their savings account. He wrote in his letter that she could have the rest. He left her papers signing over the practice and their house to her along with a letter saying he consented to a divorce."

"Wow," was all Melody could think to say.

"She said she'd never been happier. She has all the money and no husband. She said she already booked a trip to Hawaii and leaves tonight."

"How awful."

"We think maybe *she* is why he left. Obviously he was planning it for a long time since he signed over the house and everything."

"No wonder his schedule was so open for setting his deposition."

Melody expressed her condolences to Nancy who was not only losing a boss she cared for and thought she knew, but also her job. She hung up the phone in shock, wondering how she was going to break the news to Dan and their clients that their star witness had disappeared.

The record! Melody nearly ran to the conference room. *It's our only hope now,* she thought. She pulled the binder with Dr. Maerow's records from the middle of the stack. The binders on top slid like playing cards onto the table. She flipped to the divider tab labeled, "Dr. Maerow."

"MAEROW 59, MAEROW 60, MAEROW 61," she read to herself. "MAEROW 63, MAEROW 64." She turned the pages back and shuffled through them again. She rubbed page 61 between her thumb and index finger hoping number MAEROW 62 was stuck to the back. It wasn't there. She sat down and carefully looked through each piece of paper under Dr. Maerow's tab. She blew on the edge and massaged each to free the record in case it had been misplaced. She did this twice, but still no luck.

"Where could it be?" Melody muttered. "It was just here." She could feel her heart accelerating and panic creeping toward her like horror movie slime, but she didn't give up yet.

She poured through each binder, page by page, hoping to miraculously locate the record. It was a futile effort. MAEROW 62 was not there. It was gone just like Dr. Maerow had snatched it himself and took it with him on his mid-life crisis.

Dr. Maerow's office! They have the original chart. I'll just go there and pick up another copy. The panic retreated and Melody's heart slowed as a sense of relief enveloped her.

As she drove toward Dr. Maerow's office, she began to feel guilty. Nancy and her co-workers were in turmoil and she was going to ask them to do her a favor that would not benefit them at all. To soften the blow and in an effort to appear less callous, she stopped by a florist on the way to the doctor's office. She purchased a bouquet of cheerful carnations and hoped it would do the trick.

Melody walked into the waiting room at Dr. Maerow's office. It was eerily silent and empty. She looked at her watch: 2:15 p.m. She hoped they were not still at lunch or had already left for the day. *They wouldn't leave the door unlocked. They must be here*, Melody thought.

She pushed the top button of the metal bell sitting on the ledge of the check-in window counter. It rang shrill but hollow and seemed too loud. A woman, older than she but younger than her mother, came around the corner of the canvas covered wall behind the receptionist's desk. She wore blue flowered scrubs that appeared as if they'd been squashed in a tight ball wet and not opened until the fabric had completely dried. She wore a bun in her blond hair; at least Melody thought it was a bun. So many hairs had fallen from it and lay in loose strands around the woman's face, it resembled a bun perhaps Marky could've put in.

"May I help you?" The woman wiped her nose with a piece of gauze. As she came closer, Melody saw that her eyes were bloodshot and red, encircled by black where her mascara had smeared.

Melody held the flowers below the ledge of the counter where the woman would not see them. "Yes, I'm looking for Nancy."

"I'm Nancy."

"Hi, Nancy. I'm Melody Madson. We spoke on the phone this morning."

It took several seconds for Nancy to remember her, "Oh, yes. Dr. Maerow was supposed to give a deposition for you tomorrow."

"Yes."

"I'm sorry. You don't look how I'd pictured you," said Nancy.

"You thought I'd be older?" Melody smiled.

"I did, I'm sorry. You are probably not to the age yet where being told you look young is a welcome comment."

"That's okay. I get that a lot."

Nancy tugged at her shirt and tried to wipe the mascara from her eyes. "Look at me. I'm a mess. What can I do for you?"

"I was wondering if you could help me with something, and I thought you might need some cheering up so I brought these." Melody pulled the flowers up and handed them to Nancy through the check-in window.

"That's so sweet of you. Thank you. They're beautiful." Nancy sniffed the carnations and then sat the vase down onto the counter behind the window. "I don't know what I can do to help you, but I'll try."

It hadn't occurred to Melody until that moment to feel embarrassed for losing a key piece of evidence and she decided to be honest about it, "It's kind of embarrassing. We have a certain really important medical record from Dr. Maerow's chart but I'm having trouble locating it at the office."

Melody reached into her purse, pulling out the patient's waiver Candy had signed to originally allow Dr. Maerow's office to give them copies of her medical records. Luckily, Dr. Maerow hadn't required a subpoena to release them. She passed it through the window to Nancy. "So I thought I'd just stop by to get another copy from you. I just need this one note from March 22nd."

"Sure, I can do that for you. Do you just want to wait a minute? It shouldn't take very long."

"Yes. Thank you." Melody sat down in one of the chairs lined up along the wall opposite the check-in window. She grabbed a magazine from the fan arranged on the glass-topped coffee table in the middle of the waiting room floor. She turned the wrinkled brittle pages without reading any of the words or paying attention to any of the pictures. When she'd flipped the last page, she turned the magazine over to look at the cover for any articles that interested her. The headlines were unfamiliar and irrelevant to Melody. She looked at the address label and realized why; the magazine was seven years old.

She returned it to its original place in the fan and searched through the rest to find a current volume. The newest magazine was nearly two years old so Melody dismissed reading, sat back in the chair, and studied the artwork on the walls. She was beginning to think it was taking an awfully long time to copy one record when she saw Nancy approach the check-in window. Melody jumped up. As she walked toward the window, she noticed Nancy had nothing in her hands.

Nancy slid the check-in window open. The noise gave Melody goose bumps and she clenched her fists to keep herself from shivering.

"Are you sure this patient's name is spelled correctly? I'm having a hard time finding the chart."

Melody took the patient's waiver from Nancy. "Candace Carstens, C-A-R-S-T-E-N-S. That's correct."

"How about her birth date? Is that accurate?"

"Yes. I remember this birth date on the other records. Plus this is the same waiver we sent to get her records originally."

Nancy whacked her forehead with the pad of her hand. "That's right. I'm sorry. So we must have it somewhere. Let me look some more."

Melody tried to sit down but couldn't sit still, so she got up to pace the floor. She walked back and forth in the doctor's office waiting area for at least ten more minutes before Nancy came back out with a woman dressed in a business suit.

"Melody. This is my supervisor, Tracy."

"Hi."

In a raspy voice, Tracy said, "We don't have this patient's chart in our office. How quickly do you need this record?"

Melody explained the trial she needed the record for was set to begin in a week and without Dr. Maerow's testimony, she needed the record immediately.

Nancy asked, "Could Dr. Maerow have taken the chart with him?"

"Wait a second," Tracy said. "This is the patient Doctor was supposed to have the deposition about tomorrow, isn't it?"

"Yes," Melody answered.

"I remembered he did say he was going to take those records home to review over the weekend so he'd be ready for the deposition. I'll call his wife and see if he left them at home anywhere."

Tracy left the check-in window open while she called Dr. Maerow's wife. After what seemed like an hour, she finally spoke into the telephone, "Yes, Mrs. Maerow. This is Tracy from Dr. Maerow's office." There was a brief pause. Tracy bit her lip, "I'm calling because we are missing a patient's chart from the office. Doctor was to give a deposition about this patient tomorrow and we believe he may have taken the chart home with him."

"Yes, could you? We would appreciate it. The name of the patient is Candace Carstens." Nancy spelled Candy's first and last names. She put her hand over the receiver and said to Melody and Nancy, "She's going to check his office. He's always been very good about patient confidentiality, so I'm sure she will find it there."

Several minutes passed. "Really? Are you sure?" Tracy said to Dr. Maerow's wife. "Just a minute."

Tracy again covered the mouth piece and whispered, "She said there are no charts at all in his office, but she could've sworn she saw some in there over the weekend."

Nancy asked, "Why would he take them with him?"

Tracy began to answer but stopped abruptly. She held up her index finger, uncovered the receiver, and jerked it back up next to her mouth. "Oh…okay," she said. The color drained from Tracy's face.

"What is it?" Nancy asked. "Are you okay?"

Tracy struggled to regain composure. "She's just going to check one more place," she said without bothering to shield Mrs. Maerow from the conversation.

Dr. Maerow's wife returned to the telephone in a few moments.

"I see," said Tracy. "Okay. Thank you for your help, Mrs. Maerow. Yes, we are getting everything we can cleaned out right now. Have fun in Hawaii."

Melody thought she heard Mrs. Maerow's end of the phone disconnect, but several seconds elapsed before Tracy said, "Goodbye," and hung up the phone. She placed the receiver back in the telephone cradle more gently than necessary and then rested her fingers on the keypad. She stared at the phone like she had just said goodbye to the love of her life rather than the wife of her unaccounted-for boss.

"Well," said Nancy. "What did she say? Did she find the chart?"

"She did." Tracy looked up.

"That's great," said Melody. "Whew." She pretended to wipe sweat from her brow. "Is she bringing it in?"

"No," said Tracy.

"That's okay. I can go pick it up."

"No, you can't."

"I thought you said she found it."

"She did. At least she found part of it."

"I don't understand." The room was beginning to spin and it felt like the rug she was standing on was shifting beneath her. Melody leaned against the counter to steady herself. "I have the waiver. Why can't we get it?"

Tracy inhaled deeply, "Mrs. Maerow remembered after seeing Doctor's empty office that he had a fire in their fire pit yesterday. She went out to look and saw bits of paper. They were medical records."

"Was she sure Candy's records were burned?"

"Yes. It was strange she said; she looked down in the ashes and the first thing she saw was a piece of a record with 'andy Carste' on it."

Melody stepped back. The back of her knees hit the coffee table behind her. She caught herself from falling onto the table with her hands.

"I'm sorry we couldn't help you," Tracy said.

"Thanks for trying," said Melody to the floor. She sank into the nearest waiting room chair to keep from passing out. Tracy disappeared into the back of the office.

Nancy came through the patient door. She walked to Melody and touched her shoulder. "Are you okay?"

Melody absently waved her hand. "Yes, I'm fine." She got up and walked to the door. "Thanks for looking for it," she said to no one in particular.

As Melody opened the door, she heard Nancy offer, "Can I get you some water or something?" but she sounded like she was at the end of a long tunnel. Melody just vaguely shook her head, "No," and left.

She drove all the way back to her office before realizing it was after five and everyone was gone for the day. She went home without going into the office to turn off her computer or straighten her desk as she did every other day when leaving in the evening. She told her parents she wasn't feeling well and went to bed, hoping that when she woke up, she would find the events of the last eight hours had just been a nightmare.

Chapter Nineteen
Lost and Alone

The next morning, Melody sat staring at her computer screen. She didn't know what to do. The curser mocked her, flashing, waiting. She thought so hard about how the case could be won without Dr. Maerow and his record that a sharp ache spread across her forehead. It travelled to her temples and she had to close her eyes to relieve just a little of the pain, which was made worse by her office's fluorescent lights.

She struggled back and forth as to whether or not she should tell Eric. He told her he was her friend and she thought maybe he'd have an idea about what to do or at least help her feel better. But she was still embarrassed about telling him about her true feelings and thought it best to just leave him alone. She finally decided to send him an e-mail saying she was having a problem with the case and she wondered if he could help. He didn't respond. Melody knew he was there because she'd heard him walk by in the hallway outside her office, talking to another attorney.

Feeling like she had nowhere to turn, Melody called Jewel Tuesday evening, but she didn't answer so she checked Jewel's school website and found out that it was opening night for the fall drama production. Melody wondered why Jewel hadn't asked her to go to the play with her but then remembered Jewel *had* mentioned the play three weeks ago, but Melody hadn't responded. *She must have thought I didn't want to go*, she thought.

Melody went to Jewel's school's fall play on opening night every year, even when Jewel was in middle school and it was not yet "her" school. They made an elaborate evening of it, wearing their best dresses and making one of their parents take them out to dinner. This year, they could finally drive themselves and Melody remembered talking with Jewel at last year's play about how great it was going to be. The first few years, they pretended they were famous movie stars going to a Broadway show in New York City. By the time Jewel was in high school, it became a tradition and they went just for fun.

Melody felt terrible and fell asleep Tuesday night thinking about how she might make it up to Jewel. She was actually thankful to have another problem to distract her. Melody was certain that she'd lose her first case and her job.

On Wednesday, Dan called a meeting to get ready for the trial. He invited anyone to attend for free pizza for lunch to talk about how they were going to present the case to get an idea about how the jury, who also would not know anything about the case before arriving at court, might react to certain evidence and the opening statements. Because Melody had never argued in court, Dan decided it was better for someone more experienced to deliver the opening statement to layout MPOPS' view about how to interpret the evidence presented during the trial. Melody had written an opening statement weeks ago. She was disappointed at first, but then conceded to herself Dan was probably right. Now, after losing the important document, she was sure it would have been better for Dan to handle the case in every aspect, not just the opening statement.

Melody was glad the meeting was scheduled for the noon hour so she would not have to face Eric. But shortly after she got her slice of pizza and sat down, Eric arrived. When he entered the dimly lit conference room, her shoulders stiffened and her eyes sunk to the table. The knots in her stomach had already diminished her appetite but, with Eric's arrival, they tightened. Suddenly, Melody was not hungry at all and pushed her plate away. Awkwardness set in. The tension that passed between them was evident to no one else, but she knew the memory of their last encounter passed through both Eric's and her mind.

Melody stared straight ahead, avoiding Eric's glance, acting as if all was okay. She pretended she did not feel his pull, his questioning, or confusion, but she knew he was there three feet away as sure as she knew her own name. It could not be ignored or wished away. The tension was thick and muddy. Melody was sure she felt something more than friendship flowing between them, not just through a one-way avenue as Eric asserted. She thought Eric's denial was his choice and his turning away from his true self to preserve others' perceptions was not out of character for him. She consoled herself, telling herself the relationship would have never worked anyway and at least she could be proud of her honesty and integrity.

"It looks like almost everyone is finished eating so let's get started." Dan stood from the end of the long conference room table. "At the heart of this case is Midland's history, the Midland Marquee Theater, which honored magnificent spectacles from Shakespearean plays to Vaudeville musicals in its hey-day as a premier theater venue for not only Midland but the entire region." Dan continued with his proposed opening statement. Melody took notes on the audience's reaction. All seemed interested and focused on Dan; a good sign. When he was finished, he opened up the meeting for questions.

"What's this piece of evidence that will expose the plaintiff as a fraud?" asked one of the firm's corporation attorney's administrative assistants.

"Good. You caught that," said Dan, "It was my test to see if anyone would get intrigued by the promise of scandal."

"Yay! I passed!" joked the administrative assistant.

"The idea is if the jurors are intrigued, they will focus on the trial, particularly the presentation of our evidence, and not miss the key item we want them to take away."

"Okay. So are you going to tell us?" asked another assistant whose name Melody also couldn't remember.

"Thanks to our newest associate, Melody Madson," said Dan, holding his outstretched hand toward Melody, "we have a medical record from the plaintiff's doctor that is going to derail the plaintiff's entire case. This record states Ms. Carstens admitted to her doctor a refrigerator fell on her ankle the morning she allegedly fell at the theater." Melody sank into her chair, her face glowing like the burner on an electric stove. She had to tell Dan that Dr. Maerow had disappeared when he'd asked her

Tuesday afternoon how his deposition had gone, but she didn't tell him she could not find the medical record.

"I'd like everyone's opinion about something regarding the doctor and this record." Dan asked, "If the doctor was not available to testify at trial, how likely would you be to believe the record as written if the plaintiff testified she actually told her doctor after she fell, her ankle merely *felt* like a refrigerator had fallen on it?"

"It would definitely be better to hear the doctor's testimony," someone offered and asked, "Why can't he come to the trial?"

"Of course, we would have him appear live at trial if we could, but before he could be deposed, he skipped town. He ran away from his wife and his practice and is nowhere to be found." As Dan explained, it felt like rocks were piling up one by one in Melody's stomach.

Everyone at the meeting concurred that even without the doctor's confirmation of his record's authenticity as written, they would still be more likely to believe a statement written in black and white as opposed to the testimony of a plaintiff who had the obvious ulterior motive of money to lie. The weight of the imaginary rocks in Melody's stomach pulled her to the floor. Feeling sick, she excused herself from the meeting and returned to her office. She closed her door, rested her head on her desk, and wished for a miracle.

Later that afternoon, Maggie stopped by. "Are you okay, Melody?"

"I'm okay."

"Are you sure? You didn't look okay at the meeting. You didn't even eat any pizza."

"I know. I was just feeling a little tired and nauseated, I guess."

"Maybe the stress of this trial is getting to you."

Melody said, "Maybe," but thought, *Definitely*.

"You should go home. Get some rest. Trust me, it will be better for you and your work to get the rest now and come back tomorrow fresh rather than push yourself so you break at a key moment."

"Thanks, Maggie. Maybe I will go home," Melody said, although she thought it wouldn't help anything because she already broke at the key moment.

Melody e-mailed Dan and the receptionist to tell them she wasn't feeling well and was going home for the day, just in case someone asked where she was. She wondered if Eric would even realize she was not there, let alone admit he cared enough to ask about her well-being.

On Thursday, Melody spent the day hunting for the medical record under the pretense she was preparing exhibit notebooks. She studied every piece of paper at least twice, hoping perhaps she missed it because she had remembered incorrectly what it looked like. That night, she texted Jewel. When she didn't respond, she tried to call her on the Johnson's landline again. Jordan answered and initially said to a hold a minute while he gave the phone to Jewel, but when he came back, he said Jewel was unavailable.

"Okay. Thanks, Jordan. Will you just have her call me when she is *available*?"

"Sure," Jordan said. "So how have you been? I haven't seen you around in awhile."

"I've been really busy at work and I guess Jewel has been busy, too."

"Really? She seems like the same old lazy Jewel to me."

"She never answers my texts or calls to her cell phone. And every time I call your house, she is out with either Chad or some new friends from school." Jordan was quiet. "Let me guess. Jewel has not been quite the social butterfly as it would appear?"

"I'm sorry, Melody."

"That's okay. She must really be mad at me."

"What could you have possibly done to make her mad at you? I'm sure it is just Jewel being self-centered as usual."

"No. I've been neglecting her."

"But you've got a job and real responsibilities now. She should learn to understand that."

"Maybe, but it takes two to have a friendship or not have a friendship." Melody was suddenly reminded of Eric. "Will you just ask Jewel to call me? Maybe she'll be more willing if you tell her I plan to apologize."

"I will. I hope it works out; she's not nearly as fun to tease without you around."

"Thanks, Jordan." Melody laughed. "Within the next week or two I should have time to talk you out of going to law school if you're still interested."

"Talk me out of it? No way. It can't be that bad."

"I'm just having a bad week, I guess."

"I want to hear it all, the good and bad."

"You'll get that. Don't forget to tell Jewel to call me."

"I won't. Hang in there, Melody. I'm sure everything will be fine."

"Thanks. Bye."

"Bye." Melody heard Jordan disconnect and then pushed the end button on her phone. She smiled slightly, surprised that she felt a little better after talking to Jordan. She went to sleep that night knowing the next time she lay in bed trying to fall asleep, Dan would know she lost the record he was depending on to win the case and Jewel would know how sorry she was for not being the friend she wanted to be.

Chapter Twenty
Confession Number Two

When Melody got to work on Friday, she asked the receptionist to let her know as soon as Dan arrived. She thought if she was going to be fired, it was better to be fired at the beginning of the day rather than the end. She sat drumming her fingers on her desk, staring at her computer screen. She watched the minutes drag by as she waited. At 9:03, her telephone startled her. Her heart immediately began to thump, and the noise was so loud in her ears she could barely hear the receptionist say Dan had a deposition to go to and wouldn't be in until later in the afternoon. Finally, at 3:17, she was again startled by her telephone ringing, but this time, the receptionist was calling to say Dan was in.

Melody's feet were heavy as she dragged herself to Dan's office, her heart thundering, drowning out the clunk of her chunky heels on the marble floors. As she approached Dan's door, she saw him hunched over his desk, intent on a document he ferociously scribbled on in red pen.

Melody drew in a deep breath and knocked on Dan's doorframe. He looked up and said, "Hi Melody, come on in. I was just working on my opening statement. Do you want to hear it?"

She felt like a mouse, timid under Dan's cheerful gaze, and she wished she could scurry away unnoticed, but it was too late for that. Barely louder than a whisper, she said, "Before we do that, there's something I need to talk to you about if you have a minute."

"Of course. Have a seat." Dan dropped his pen onto his legal pad with a thud. He leaned toward Melody and then got up, walked around his desk, and sat down in the empty chair next to Melody. He bounced the chair, turning it to face her squarely. "Are you feeling okay?"

"Yes, I'm okay," said Melody and then she spit out, "The record from Dr. Maerow's chart, the one saying a refrigerator fell on Candace, the one we need for trial, is missing." Melody looked at her hands clutched tightly in her lap, her knuckles white as she tried to suppress her tears.

Dan was silent. He sat opposite from her with nothing between them but dead air. He bent his left leg up to rest on the top of his right knee. He leaned on his elbow and roughly rubbed his chin.

"I had the record in our binders but when I went to get it out, it was gone. I looked all over for it and tried to get it from Dr. Maerow's office but he burned her chart before he left. And they don't have anything electronic. I'm so sorry," Melody said in one breath. A dark shadow speckled with glitter narrowed her vision and she had to close her eyes to keep from passing out.

"So let's see if I understand you correctly," said Dan.

Melody shook her head in agreement.

"We had the record stating the plaintiff admitted to her doctor the injuries for which the Midland Marquee Theater building is at risk of being demolished was not caused by her fall at the building but by her own refrigerator falling on it. Right?"

Melody whispered, "Yes."

"And now the doctor who made that record is missing and the record, the only thing we had to save the building, is not only missing from our file, but is also missing from the doctor's office?"

Melody clenched her teeth.

"Do I have that right?" asked Dan.

"Yeh-es." Melody choked. She could not will her tears back any longer. They began to fall, sliding down both her cheeks and dripping onto her lap. Dan reached across his desk and pulled a tissue from the box on the corner. Melody noticed the tissue that sprung up behind the one Dan had pulled out was much darker in color, but she knew she didn't have the luxury of non-sun-faded tissues and probably didn't deserve them anyway. She dabbed the clear drainage from her upper lip and held her breath to try to stop her tears. The harder she tried to stop crying, the fiercer her tears flowed. She folded the saturated tissue, trying to find a dry spot. All she wanted was the moment to be over and she did not want to prolong it by asking for another tissue.

Dan cleared his throat, grabbed the entire box of tissues and sat it in Melody's lap. The dust on the top of the box tickled her nose. She put a fresh tissue to it just in time to prevent a shot of mucous flying from her nose with a sneeze. Normally, it would have made her eyes water, but her tear ducts were already pouring wide open so it didn't make any difference. When she finally gained enough control of herself to face Dan, she looked up and saw him staring at the ceiling, his head flung back unnaturally over the back of the chair. He looked headless and she feared she'd shocked him unconscious.

Melody stared at the rain falling against the window behind Dan's desk. He finally lifted his head and squeezed his eyes tightly shut before finally speaking. "I guess that's that."

"So I'm fired?"

"I mean that's it for the case. It's over. Without that record, I'll have to drop the case, which will allow the settlement to go through and the building to be torn down unless we can think of another way to argue the case." Dan knocked on the stack of magazines on his desk. "You didn't find anything showing Harrison affirmatively kept up with repair and maintenance, did you?"

"No, we looked through all of those boxes of documents in the theater's basement and weren't able to find anything." Melody bit her lip. "Could we argue Harrison has the responsibility for proving he did the maintenance and repairs?"

"We have the burden of proof but there might be a way to turn the tables. But it's a long shot and would take a lot of research." Dan looked at his watch. "Everyone is probably gone for the day and I'm going out of town this weekend."

"I'll do it."

"Are you sure you haven't done enough?" Melody looked back down at her lap, her tears threatening to let loose again. "I'm sorry, Melody. I'm not saying you will be working here after the personnel committee meets in a couple of weeks, but it's not over until the judge cracks his gavel announcing, 'Case dismissed,' and even then, there's the appeal process, although I don't think that will help in this case."

"I'll do anything to fix this. I've never messed up anything this important this badly before."

"It is a big mistake, but we've all made them."

"But on the first case I've ever worked on and something as simple as hanging onto a piece of paper? I'd fire me."

Dan took the tissue box from Melody's hands and sat it on his desk. "Let's not get ahead of ourselves, okay? It's not over yet. An attorney is never 100% prepared for a trial until he walks in the courtroom; usually you're closer than this, but still, it's not over. See what you can come up with. If you find something you think will work, call me on my cell phone; otherwise I'll be here early Monday morning to make the final decision."

"And if I don't come up with anything?"

"Then we'll talk to our clients and I'll likely recommend they drop the case."

"Then I won't be welcome here any longer?"

"The personnel committee meets a week from next Thursday. They'll review everything, maybe ask you some questions, and then they'll decide. It's hard to predict which way they'll go. You're a bright attorney and I'm sure you'll never make the same mistake again, but this is a pretty big case for the firm and losing it could cost us a lot of money, not only from MPOPs as an organization, but any legal services any of the members need individually."

185

"I understand." Melody resigned herself to potentially leaving her fate in the hands of people she barely knew.

Dan rose from the chair and walked slowly to the other side of his desk, pausing briefly to look out the window. He turned toward Melody, his hands on his sides, resting on top of his black leather belt, "Personally, I'm inclined to recommend you stay. You are bright, I think you have the potential to be a great attorney, and I don't believe in stomping out a career based on one mistake this early. But the committee might not agree."

He turned back to the window, leaned his head into the glass, and looked to the street below. He sat back into his desk chair and picked up his pen.

Melody said, "I'll be here all weekend to try to find something to fix what I've done."

"I'm sure you'll do your best. Remember, call me if you find anything."

"I will." Melody bumped her knee on the chair's oak arm and clenched her hands to keep from blurting, "Ouch." She turned back to tell Dan thank you for giving her the chance to work on the case, but he had already picked up his phone and was dialing. Not wanting to know who he was calling or what he was going to say, Melody rushed back to her office.

She called home to leave a message letting her family know she would be late getting home from work that night and then typed a long email apology to Jewel. She was just about to push send when Eric appeared in her doorway. She pretended she hadn't noticed he was there and thought, *Great. This is the last thing I need now.*

She hoped Eric would pick up her hint and leave, but he cleared his throat so Melody could not ignore him. She looked up toward him, still typing, but nothing comprehendible. "I'm sorry but I'm really busy," she said.

"I know. I just talked to my dad."

Melody resumed her effort of ignoring Eric.

"I won't keep you. I just wanted to say goodbye."

"Goodbye," said Melody. "Have a good weekend," she added in reflex.

"I'm not coming back."

Melody's hands froze in mid-type. "Oh," was all she could say.

"I decided to focus more on the Heartstring Rockets."

"That's great." Melody pretended she was happy for him. Maybe one day she would be happy for him, but right now there was no room for anyone's problems but her own.

"I finally stood up to my parents."

"Good for you."

"I told them I was never going to want to be a lawyer so it was a waste of time for me to be here every afternoon and I refused to come back after today."

Melody smiled at Eric meekly. "I hope it works out for you."

"I hope everything works out for you, too, Melody. Not just with what is going on now but with everything else, too."

"Thanks." Melody sensed Eric was about to say something more and she was sure she was too humiliated to hear it, so before he could open his mouth, Melody said, "Nothing is going to work out if I don't get to work, so I'd better get back at it." She pointed to her computer screen.

Eric hesitated and Melody held her breath, afraid he would forge ahead with whatever it was he wanted to say, but he gently slapped her doorframe with his right hand before waving slightly and disappearing from her office and her life. She still didn't know if he was denying his feelings or if he never felt them, but it no longer mattered. She had learned that she couldn't always control her feelings, but she could be honest about them. She knew one day she would meet a boy without a girlfriend who was also available emotionally. Now Melody's only worries were if she would be able to save her case and her friendship with Jewel. She hoped her e-mail apology would work.

Chapter Twenty-One
Discovery

Melody got home from work Friday night at midnight. She awoke at 4:30 a.m., and, unable to fall back to sleep, she decided at 5:30 to just get up. Her parents and Marky were in bed asleep when she got home, and since it was Saturday, they were still asleep when Melody left the house at 5:50 a.m. She wrote a note to let them know she was home but had gone back to work on the upcoming trial. She told her parents the trial's start date when it was moved up a couple of weeks ago and they noted it on the calendar. She wasn't strong enough to tell them she had messed up the case and was about to mess up her entire career. They were so proud of her; she didn't want to disappoint them. As they did several days in advance of final exams, they let her prepare. After so many years, they trusted Melody knew what was best; she must because whatever she did always worked. Melody was more grateful than ever for this courtesy and relied on being in denial with them at least until Monday evening after the trial should have begun.

She locked herself in her office all weekend, researching statutes and decisions from past cases to try to find another argument to launch on behalf of Midland Preserve Our Past Society to save the Midland Marquee Theater. MPOPS had tried to list the building on the National Register of Historic Places, but without Ron Harrison's consent as the owner, they were prohibited from adding it to the list. The organization was not able to raise the million dollars Harrison demanded as a selling price for the building or the several hundred thousand additional dollars required to renovate the building if they were able to purchase it. The entire case hinged on nullifying the settlement agreement between Carstens and Harrison. The only way to render the settlement invalid would be to prove Harrison and the Midland Marquee Theater were not responsible for Carstens' injury. The only evidence of that would be testimony or a document indicating Carstens' broken ankle was caused by something other than her fall in the theater. The only hope for that had left town, been misplaced, and burned, and no matter what search terms she used or what artery of research she followed down through the smallest capillaries, Melody could not avoid those facts.

It was after four o'clock Sunday afternoon. Her research kept circling her back to the same statutes and case decisions. "It's no use," she said. Confident that she had seen every bit of legal information available about historic buildings, slip and falls, demolition, contracts, settlement agreements, injunctions, and evidence, she shut down her computer.

On her way out, she walked past Maggie's office. As she did, she noticed the light was on; it was off when she walked by earlier in the day. When she went in to see if Maggie was there, she noticed several hanging folders sticking out from Maggie's open filing cabinet drawer.

"Maggie?" As she began to straighten the files so she could close the drawer, she saw a familiar paper lying on the bottom. She pulled it out. "The record," she said.

Hearing the door slam, she looked up to find Maggie and another girl standing in the room.

"Find what you were looking for?" Maggie asked.

"How did this get here?"

"You're the smart one," Maggie poked her index finger into the other girl's side. "You tell us how it got there." Maggie then pointed her finger at Melody. The other girl looked familiar and Melody tried to remember where she had seen her before.

"You remember me?" the other girl asked. "You stole valedictorian from me, remember? And now you've fallen in my trap. Not so clever after all, are we?"

"Suzie?"

"That's right. Didn't recognize me with my new short, red hairdo, did you?"

"What are you doing here?" Melody reached for the door handle but Maggie and Suzie jumped in front of it, blocking her escape.

"I'm here to teach you a lesson." Suzie pulled a yellow braided plastic rope from behind her back. "You took something away from me so I'm here to take something away from you."

Melody turned her attention to Maggie, "But why would you help Suzie? I thought we were friends?"

"So smart, yet so naïve." Maggie lunged for Melody, grabbing her arms. Suzie grabbed Melody's feet and forced her to sit in Maggie's office chair. Melody struggled, but she couldn't break free from the other girls. They tied her arms to the armrests and her feet to the base. Hoping someone else was in the building,

Melody screamed as loud as she could, but, before she could attract any attention, Suzie tied a long strip of cloth over her mouth between her jaws.

Maggie leaned on Melody's arms tied to the chair; she put all of her weight on them and Melody started to cry from the crushing pain.

"You think you are such a hot shot." Maggie shoved her face so close to Melody's, she could feel Maggie's breath. It smelled like mints and garlic. "You come in here and think you can just take over." She pushed Melody away from her and stood up. "Suzie is my cousin. She told me about you; about how you just walked into senior year and took valedictorian away from her, something she'd worked for her whole life."

Maggie crossed her arms in front of her chest and sneered at Melody. "When you started working here, I thought you were just a little girl; there was no way you could steal anything. But then you stole Dan, you stole Eric, and you stole my case, so I decided Suzie was right. We got together and decided to steal something from you."

Melody tried to stretch her toes to the floor so she could wheel herself toward the telephone, but the chair just spun in circles.

"We came up with this plan to ruin you and your case. We knew you'd be here this weekend to try to save your little soul. But you wouldn't and then Maggie could show up, having found the precious medical record *you* lost, and save the day," Suzie said.

192

Melody tried to yell out around her gag. Suzie pulled the fabric down from Melody's mouth, scratching her lip.

"What are you going to do with me?" Melody choked.

Suzie replaced the gag and looked at Maggie. "So what are we going to do with her?" she asked.

"I don't know," Maggie answered. Suzie and Maggie left the room, closing the heavy wood door behind them. Melody rocked the chair back and forth, trying to walk it over to the phone or the sharp edge of Maggie's metal desk so she could cut the rope. After what seemed like an eternity, Melody heard her cell phone ringing in her bag on the floor next to the door where she had dropped it. The phone rang twice before Melody noticed the door's brass knob slowly turning. She held her breath, fearing what Suzie and Maggie had decided to do to her.

The door crept open and a head cautiously peered through the narrow opening. *Jewel!* As soon as Jewel saw Melody, she swung the door open and ran toward her. She untied the gag. "What happened? Are you okay?"

Melody shook her head no and covered her mouth with cupped hands to try to keep from hyperventilating. Melody explained to Jewel what Maggie and Suzie had done. Jewel reached for the rope to release Melody from the chair. Suzie burst through the door.

"Look here." Suzie waved Maggie into the room. "She's got a little friend who thinks she's going to save her." Suzie and Maggie shoved Melody to the side of the chair and squeezed

Jewel down next to her. They tied Jewel to Melody and the chair. They re-gagged Melody but didn't have anything to quiet Jewel.

Maggie said, "We need to get them out of here." She and Suzie pushed the girls in the chair to the elevator and out of the building into a cleaned out utility van. As they drove away, the chair rolled down the back and slammed into the doors. Melody feared they would pop open, plunging them into the street.

After several minutes of bouncing and rolling into the van's side walls, the vehicle slowed and stopped.

"What are they doing?" Jewel whispered. Suzie and Maggie got out of the van. They heard two car doors slam and the motor of whatever they had got into, speed off. Jewel and Melody were quiet for a long time, listening intently to see if Suzie or Maggie would come back, fearing what they would do with them if they did come back.

The van darkened as the sun set. "I don't think they're coming back." Jewel strained her neck and used her teeth to untie the fabric strip binding Melody's mouth. She spit out the cloth and tried to moisten her dried-out mouth by swishing her saliva.

"I'm so sorry." Melody began to sob. "How did you know where to find me?"

"I got your e-mail. You said you were coming over, but when you didn't show up, I got worried and decided to come looking for you."

Melody told Jewel the rest of the story through the darkness of the van. She told her she thought she had lost the only piece of paper that might help her firm win the case and because of her, they were going to tear down an entire building. Melody even told her about Eric, her feelings for him, and how she humiliated herself by telling Eric about them. Jewel confessed she and Chad had broken up, but she didn't want to tell Melody that she had failed at the only thing she was better at than Melody: dating.

"What are we going to do, Jewel?" The heat from the van's furnace had long dissipated and the warmth generated by huddling so close to Jewel was beginning to fail. "We'll freeze to death."

"There's got to be something we can do." Jewel chewed her top lip.

"It's hopeless," said Melody, her words creating a cloud in the cold air.

"No, it's not. I have my phone in my pocket; I put it in there when I saw you in that room."

"So when you miss curfew, your parents can track your phone."

"Well...," Jewel said. "Actually, I turned that off the other day when I got mad at my mom."

"Great. Then it's not going to do us any good in your pocket."

"Maybe we can maneuver around these ropes to try to push the buttons. It doesn't matter which buttons, we can just yell to whoever answers to call the police and hope they can hear it through my jeans."

The girls twisted their arms to try to untangle them from the ropes. Finally, with their arms in a contorted pretzel, Melody was able to stretch her elbow toward the cell phone in Jewel's pocket. She pushed her elbow into the cell phone.

"Ouch!" Jewel said. Melody could see the sparkle of tears in her eyes.

"Sorry."

"That's okay. Just hurry," Jewel said through clenched teeth.

At last they heard ringing.

"We got someone." They waited. Melody feared their call would go to voice mail but a familiar voice answered.

"Jordan!" they cried in unison.

"Jewel, is that you? What are you doing? You better get home. Do you know how late it is?"

"Jordan, you need to help us! We've been kidnapped!"

"Stop messing around, Jewel, and get home."

"I'm not kidding, Jordan. Melody is here and we've been kidnapped."

"Yeah, right. Of all the stories you've concocted, this one has got to be…"

Before he could finish, Melody spoke up, "It's true, Jordan. Maggie from work and Suzie Sexton, the valedictorian runner-up in my class, stole a medical record from my case and when I found it, they tied me up. Jewel found me but they tied her up, put us in a van, and drove us somewhere. They left and we don't know where we are."

"I'm calling the police."

"No," Jewel said. "I'm scared. Don't hang up."

"Besides, we don't have to time to wait for police," Melody said. "We need you to find us."

"Okay. Stay on the phone. I'll try. Tell me everything you remember. Tell me everything you can see and hear."

"Hurry, Jordan, I don't have much battery left. I forgot to charge my phone again. And it's freezing!"

"Hang in there, I'm coming."

Jordan stayed on the line, describing his location while they attempted to direct him with their memories of the turns and speed of the van as it brought them there. The girls shivered. The light in the van darkened deeper and then began to soften as dawn approached. Beeps from Jewel's phone, signaling it was about to shut down, became more frequent and insistent as the light coming into the van brightened. Melody was about to succumb to cold and exhaustion when she heard a motor in the distance.

"I think I see…" the phone died before Jordan finished. Within a few seconds, the back doors flew open. Jordan rushed in and released Melody and Jewel. He hugged them both. Melody melted in Jordan's arms.

Chapter Twenty-Two
Salvation

"What time is it?" Melody pulled away from Jordan's embrace. "It's so bright out." They got out of the back of the van, squinting.

Melody noticed Jordan's cell phone on the ground. "8:30!" She grabbed the phone and ran toward his car, dialing. "Let's go!"

"Slow down. We need to wait for the police. You're not thinking straight," said Jordan.

"I'm not calling the police." Jewel and Jordan gave each other confused glances and followed Melody to the car. "I need to call work."

"What's going on?" Jordan put his car in gear and backed away from the van.

"Just drive me to the office."

Melody tried to call Dan's direct line. There was no answer. She slapped her phone's virtual number pad. She tried to call Dan on his cell phone. "This is Dan Marshdon." Melody began to interrupt him but he kept talking, "I can't answer my phone right now." Without leaving a message, she hung up. Her only option to reach Dan now was through the general number. She dialed the office number for Lazlo, Marshdon and Brown and hoped the receptionist was in to answer her call. "Pick up, pick up," she said.

"Good morning, Lazlo, Marshdon and Brown, how may I…"

Melody didn't let her finish. "I'm sorry. This is Melody. I need to speak to Dan Marshdon. It's an emergency. Is he there?"

"No. He e-mailed me from home this morning, saying he was going to go right to court. Can I put you through to his voice mail?"

"I already left him a message on his cell phone."

"He probably has it turned off. The attorneys will usually do that when they are preparing for court so they don't lose their train of thought."

Melody blankly thanked the receptionist and hung up before waiting for her goodbye. She looked at Jordan's car's clock. *8:45.*

"I have to get that record to Dan."

"Why don't you just go straight to the courthouse?" asked Jewel.

"That record was sitting on Maggie's desk right before you came in. I hope I can get it before she takes it to Dan and plays the hero."

"Oh, there's no chance of that."

"What are you talking about?" Melody swung her head toward the back seat. "She's had hours to get that record and get her story straight."

"You mean this record?" Jewel pulled a crumpled white paper from under her shirt.

Melody tore the paper from Jewel's hand. "How did you get that?"

"When Suzie came in, I saw her look at that piece of paper on the desk, and I figured it was important. So I grabbed it and stuffed it in my bra right before they grabbed me and tied me up."

Melody smoothed it out on the car seat between her and Jordan.

"So to the courthouse then?" Jordan grabbed Melody's hand.

"To the courthouse." When they got downtown, Melody was thankful most everyone out driving around on a Monday morning was already where they needed to be for the day. Jordan drove straight to the courthouse and parked in the first open space he saw.

As Melody ran in, her reflection in the glass in the courthouse doors reminded her she had been up all night and hadn't brushed her hair. She raked her hand through it but there were too many knots. She shook the hairs she'd pulled out from her hand and settled for smoothing the top layer with her palm.

The courthouse was busy with jurors arriving for the several trials scheduled to start on Monday morning. Melody got in line behind a man between the age of her father and grandfathers. He was dressed in denim overalls and wore a baseball cap. She looked at her watch. The face had cracked in the struggle with Maggie and Suzie, but she could still read the time: *9:05.*

The man ahead of her went through the security station. It took several passes through the metal detector before he had emptied all of the keys, change, and his utility tool from his pockets. The security officer gave the man a box and index card.

He told him to put his name on the card and then they would hold his knife until he left.

9:07. The guard pulled the man aside as he listed the items not allowed in the courthouse, a knife on a utility tool being at the top of the list. Melody had nothing with her except the medical record she needed to get to Dan, so she flew through the security checkpoint.

"Thank you," she breathed to the guard, walking as fast as she could without running to the stairs leading up to the courtrooms. *9:08.* She ran up the stairs and to the assignment board on the other side of the landing at the top.

Midland Preserve Our Past Society v. Candace Carstens, she read, skipping the rest of the caption, *Courtroom C*. She turned and examined the signs on the doors nearest to her. Courtroom A was ahead of her to her left and to its right was Courtroom B. She hurried to the next door. *Courtroom C*, she read and flung open the door.

The door was not as heavy as it appeared. It swung open easily and hit the bench behind it with a loud bang. The courtroom was nearly empty, but everyone there turned and stared at her. The judge sat at the front of the room on a platform behind a wide podium high above the rest of the room. Two dark tables faced the front of the judge's bench. A red-haired woman in a bright red strapless dress, a man dressed in khakis and a flannel shirt, and two men in suits, who Melody recognized as Candy, Ron, and their respective attorneys, sat at the table facing the judge on her left. Dan stood at the table on Melody's right with a handful of people she assumed represented MPOPS sitting on the benches behind the short wall separating the gallery from the participants.

The judge was dressed in a black robe, her long gray hair falling below her shoulders. She peered at Melody through thick glasses.

"Excuse me, Judge," said Dan. Melody scurried down the aisle separating the columns of benches bolted to the floor. She tripped on a loose thread in the carpet and caught herself on the swinging door on the short wall. It swung both ways and pushed in toward the judge's bench. She tripped, landing on her knee. She heard Candy giggle behind her.

"What is it? I was just about to tell the judge to dismiss the case," Dan whispered to Melody.

Melody's heart fell. "I found the missing record," she whispered, lifting herself to a standing position. "Am I too late?"

Dan turned toward the judge, "Judge, I beg your pardon. Would you please indulge me in a short break?"

The judge sighed and said hoarsely, "We're recessed for five minutes." She lifted her gavel and hammered the block.

Melody gave the record to Dan. He took it and then motioned her to follow him. They left the courtroom. When the door banged shut, Dan asked, "Why didn't you call me?"

"I was tied up, and by the time I was able to call you this morning, you were already here." Melody held her hands to her rumbling abdomen. "Am I too late?"

"No, you're right on time but with not a second to spare. Where did you find it?" Scanning Melody's disheveled clothes, he asked, "Are you okay?"

"I'm fine. It was in Maggie's desk drawer. She stole it."

"How did you get it?"

"It's a long story and we don't have time. After this, I will tell everything to you and the police."

"I don't understand." Dan shook his head in disbelief. He pulled his antiquated cell phone from his suit jacket's inside pocket. He pushed the power button and tapped his foot impatiently while he waited for it to power up. Melody wondered who he was calling. He dialed, continuing to tap his foot on the courthouse's vinyl floor.

"Sarah, this is Dan Marshdon. I need to speak with Mr. Lazlo right away."

Dan explained to Mr. Lazlo what Maggie had done. He was silent for a few seconds. She heard a click and then Mr. Lazlo faintly say, "Are you still there?"

"Yes, are we on speaker now?" Dan asked. Almost immediately, Melody heard sobs in Dan's phone. She heard Maggie say something but couldn't make out what it was. Dan's phone went quiet again as the speaker phone was switched off, and Mr. Lazlo spoke with Dan through the receiver.

"I agree, but don't let her leave. I don't have time to get into it right now, but there is more to the story than just the stolen record," said Dan. He held the power button on his phone; a short jingle sounded before it went quiet, and he snapped it shut.

Dan reached in to return his phone to the pocket inside his suit coat. He sat down in one of the chairs lined up along the hallway wall. He rubbed his eyes with the backs of his index and ring fingers.

Melody quietly sat down in the chair next to him. A few moments later, the courtroom door swung open. A friendly looking lady wearing a badge stating "Court Administrator" peered around the aluminum door. "Are you ready? Judge Atkinson is waiting."

"Yes, I'll be right in. Thank you." Dan slapped his knees with both hands and stood up.

"Now what?" Melody asked.

"You still remember the opening statement you wrote a few weeks ago?"

"Yes, but I've never argued in court before, and you said someone more experienced needed to give the opening statement."

"Forget what I said. You saved the case. You should give the opening statement."

"Really?" Melody's heart began beating with anxiety and excitement. "Do you think I could do it?"

"I think you could probably argue this case with your eyes closed." Dan pulled the door open. A cool blast of air spilled into the hallway. "Are you up for it?"

"Yes."

Melody walked through the door, holding her head high. She walked to the front of the room and held open the gallery door for

Dan. They stood behind the table as the judge entered from a side door behind the bench. Melody smiled at the judge, thinking maybe she *could* be a successful sixteen-year old lawyer after all.

Judge Atkinson sat down and pulled her chair forward before saying, "Be seated."

Dan said, "Your honor, thank you for your indulgence. We've had a slight change in plans. My associate here, Melody Madson, is going to deliver Midland Preserve Our Past Society's opening statement."

"Very well." The judge motioned to the court bailiff and he opened the door behind the judge's bench on the wall opposite from where Judge Atkinson entered. Two rows of six individuals varying in age from just a few years older than Melody to the age of her grandparents walked in and sat down in the rows of chairs waiting for them.

Judge Atkinson put on her glasses and nestled back into her oversized chair and said, "Proceed."

Melody stood up, quietly cleared her throat, and took a deep breath. As she turned away from the table to stand in front of the jury, she saw Jewel and Jordan sitting at the back of the courtroom. Jewel gave her a thumbs-up sign. Jordan just looked deep into her eyes and smiled. She smiled back and thought maybe what she'd been looking for had been right there all along. Feeling Jordan's strength and the support of her friends, Melody laid her hands on top of the lectern facing the jury and said, "Melody Madson. May it please the court?"

Epilogue
Justice

"The jury has spoken. This case is decided in favor of Midland Preserve Our Past Society. The settlement reached in Carstens v. Harrison and Midland Marquee Theater is hereby vacated and rendered null and void. The permit for demolition is hereby also vacated and the parties will proceed according to Midland's Historic Preservation Ordinance. The theater, for now, has been saved. And I personally hope MPOPS and Mr. Harrison can work something out to save it for good. Case Dismissed." Judge Atkinson slammed her gavel. The gallery stood as she descended the bench and exited the courtroom.

Melody let out a sigh of relief, thinking back over the past few days. When the trial recessed that first day, Dan, with Melody rushing behind, raced back to L, M and B. Melody waited on the floor next to the door of Frank Smith's office, her knees pulled tight to her chest. She couldn't hear much of the conversation with Maggie, the senior partners, and the police, but she wanted to be there to find out what was going to happen at the first possible moment. Finally, the door opened and the police pushed Maggie out ahead of them, her hands fastened behind her back with handcuffs.

One of the officers spoke into his radio, "Yes, that's right. Suzie Sexton. Great. Thank you." He turned to the other officer who held onto Maggie by the chain between the handcuffs. "They got the other one and will meet us at the station."

They learned later that Maggie and Suzie confessed to everything. Dr. Maerow had been Maggie's client at the firm she worked for briefly before joining Lazlo, Marshdon and Brown. While working on his case, Maggie learned that Dr. Maerow had been falsifying his medical records so he could get insurance to pay for treatment he never provided to patients, but Maggie, bound by attorney-client confidentiality, didn't turn him in. After she and Suzie put two-and-two together about who Melody was and they decided they needed to exact revenge on her, Maggie convinced Dr. Maerow she could turn him in to authorities without penalty. She blackmailed him into burning his medical records and leaving town to start over elsewhere. Maggie and Suzie were arrested for kidnapping and risked spending several years in jail.

Shaking herself back to the present, Melody turned. Tears filled her eyes as she smiled at Jewel and Jordan who talked their teachers into letting them miss school to attend the trial as a learning experience. They'd been there every day, but Melody hadn't had much of a chance to talk to them. They had their four thumbs up and huge grins; Jewel shuffled her feet like a football player at practice.

Running down the aisle, Melody spread her arms wide and threw them around Jewel. Before she realized what was happening, Jordan pulled her away, hugging her and then kissing her square on the lips. Melody's lips tingled and she touched them with her fingertips, excited to resume her best friendship with

Jewel and about the prospect of future Jordan-induced tingling lips.

CPSIA information can be obtained
at www.ICGtesting.com
Printed in the USA
FFOW02n1808250614
6080FF